ENGLISH MEN OF LETTERS

EDITED BY JOHN MORLEY

DICKENS

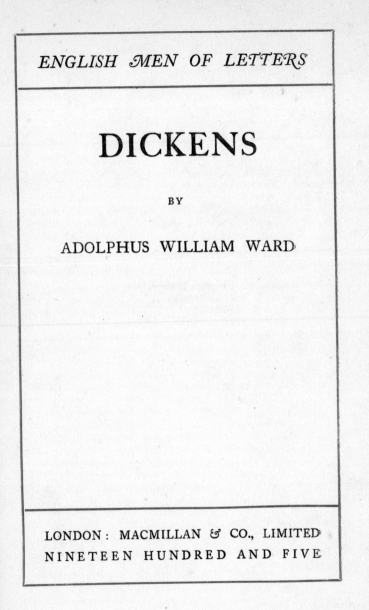

ENGLISH MEN OF LETTERS

DICKENS

BY

ADOLPHUS WILLIAM WARD

LONDON: MACMILLAN & CO., LIMITED
NINETEEN HUNDRED AND FIVE

First published 1882
Reissue 1902
Reprinted 1905

PREFACE.

AT the close of a letter addressed by Dickens to his friend John Forster, but not to be found in the English editions of the *Life*, the writer adds to his praises of the biography of Goldsmith these memorable words : " I desire no better for my fame, when my personal dustiness shall be past the control of my love of order, than such a biographer and such a critic." Dickens was a man of few close friend-ships—"his breast," he said, "would not hold many people ;" but of these friendships, that with Forster was one of the earliest, as it was one of the most enduring. To Dickens at least his future biographer must have been the embodiment of two qualities rarely combined in equal measure—discretion and candour. In literary matters his advice was taken almost as often as it was given, and nearly every proof-sheet of nearly every work of Dickens passed through his faithful helpmate's hands. Nor were there many important decisions formed by Dickens con-cerning himself in the course of his manhood, to which Forster was a stranger, though, unhappily, he more than once counselled in vain.

On Mr. Forster's *Life of Charles Dickens*, together with the three volumes of *Letters* collected by Dickens' eldest daughter and his sister-in-law—his " dearest and best friend "—it is superfluous to state that the biographical portion of the following essay is mainly based. It may also be superfluous, but it cannot be considered impertinent, if I add that the shortcomings of the *Life* have, in my opinion, been more frequently proclaimed than defined; and that its merits are those of its author as well as of its subject.

My sincere thanks are due for various favours shown to me in connexion with the production of this little volume by

Miss Hogarth, Mr. Charles Dickens, Professor Henry Morley, Mr. Alexander Ireland, Mr. John Evans, Mr. Robinson, and Mr. Britton. Mr. Evans has kindly enabled me to correct some inaccuracies in Mr. Forster's account of Dickens' early Chatham days on unimpeachable first-hand evidence. I also beg Captain and Mrs. Budden to accept my thanks for allowing me to see Gad's Hill Place.

I am under special obligations to Mr. R. F. Sketchley, Librarian of the Dyce and Forster Libraries at South Kensington, for his courtesy in affording me much useful aid and information. With the kind permission of Mrs. Forster, Mr. Sketchley enabled me to supplement the records of Dickens' life, in the period 1838–1841, from a hitherto unpublished source—a series of brief entries by him in four volumes of *The Law and Commercial Daily Remembrancer* for those years. These volumes formed no part of the Forster bequest, but were added to it, under certain conditions, by Mrs. Forster. The entries are mostly very brief; and sometimes there are months without an entry. Many days succeed one another with no other note than " Work."

Mr. R. H. Shepherd's *Bibliography of Dickens* has been of considerable service to me. May I take this opportunity of commending to my readers, as a charming reminiscence of the connexion between *Charles Dickens and Rochester*, Mr. Robert Langton's sketches illustrating a paper recently printed by him under that title ?

Last, not least, as the Germans say, I wish to thank my friend Professor T. N. Toller for the friendly counsel which has not been wanting to me on this, any more than on former occasions.

A. W. W.

Manchester, March 1882.

CONTENTS.

the very first number of *Pickwick*, epitomised the an-
tiquities and comforts of Rochester, already the scene
of one of the *Sketches*, Dickens returned to the local
associations of his early childhood. It was at Chatham
that poor little David Copperfield, on his solitary
tramp to Dover, slept his Sunday night's sleep "near
a cannon, happy in the society of the sentry's foot-
steps;" and in many a Christmas narrative or uncommercial etching the familiar features of town and
country, of road and river, were reproduced, before in
Great Expectations they suggested some of the most
picturesque effects of his later art, and before in his last
unfinished romance his faithful fancy once more haunted
the well-known precincts. During the last thirteen years
of his life he was again an inhabitant of the loved neighbourhood where, with the companions of his mirthful
idleness, he had so often made holiday; where, when
hope was young, he had spent his honeymoon; and
whither, after his last restless wanderings, he was to
return, to seek such repose as he would allow himself,
and to die. But, of course, the daily life of the
"very queer small boy" of that early time is only
quite incidentally to be associated with the grand
gentleman's house on Gad's Hill, where his father,
little thinking that his son was to act over again the
story of Warren Hastings and Daylesford, had told
him he might some day come to live, if he were to
be very persevering, and to work hard. The family
abode was in Ordnance (not St. Mary's) Place at
Chatham, amidst surroundings classified in Mr. Pickwick's
notes as "appearing to be soldiers, sailors, Jews, chalk,
shrimps, offices, and dockyard men." But though the
half-mean half-picturesque aspect of the Chatham streets

may already at an early age have had its fascination for
Dickens, yet his childish fancy was fed as fully as were
his powers of observation. Having learnt reading from his
mother, he was sent with his elder sister, Fanny, to a day-
school kept in Gibraltar Place, New Road, by Mr. William
Giles, the eldest son and namesake of a worthy Baptist
Minister, whose family had formed an intimate acquaintance with their neighbours in Ordnance Row. The younger
Giles children were pupils at the school of their elder
brother with Charles and Fanny Dickens, and thus
naturally their constant playmates. In later life, Dickens
preserved a grateful remembrance, at times refreshed
by pleasant communications between the families, of the
training he had received from Mr. William Giles, an
intelligent as well as generous man, who, recognising his
pupil's abilities, seems to have resolved that they should
not lie fallow for want of early cultivation. Nor does
there appear to be the slightest reason for supposing that
this period of his life was anything but happy. For his sister
Fanny he always preserved a tender regard ; and a touching
little paper, written by him after her death in womanhood,
relates how the two children used to watch the stars together, and make friends with one in particular, as belonging
to themselves. But obviously he did not lack playmates
of his own sex ; and it was no doubt chiefly because his
tastes made him disinclined to take much part in the
rougher sports of his schoolfellows, that he found plenty
of time for amusing himself in his own way. And thus
it came to pass that already as a child he followed his own
likings in the two directions from which they were never
very materially to swerve. He once said of himself that
he had been "a writer when a mere baby, an actor always."

Of these two passions he could always, as a child and

But these pleasant early days came to a sudden end. In the year 1821 his family returned to London, and soon his experiences of trouble began. Misfortune pursued the elder Dickens to town, his salary having been decreased already at Chatham in consequence of one of the early efforts at economical reform. He found a shabby home for his family in Bayham Street, Camden Town ; and here, what with the pecuniary embarrassments in which he was perennially involved, and what with the easy disposition with which he was blessed by way of compensation, he allowed his son's education to take care of itself. John Dickens appears to have been an honourable as well as a kindly man. His son always entertained an affectionate regard for him, and carefully arranged for the comfort of his latter years ; nor would it be fair, because of a similarity in their experiences, and in the grandeur of their habitual phraseology, to identify him absolutely with the immortal Mr. Micawber. Still less, except in certain details of manner and incident, can the character of the elder Dickens be thought to have suggested that of the pitiful "Father of the Marshalsea," to which prison, almost as famous in English fiction as it is in English history, the unlucky navy-clerk was consigned a year after his return to London.

Every effort had been made to stave off the evil day ; and little Charles, whose eyes were always wide open, and who had begun to write descriptive sketches of odd personages among his acquaintance, had become familiar with the inside of a pawnbroker's shop, and had sold the paternal "library" piecemeal to the original of the drunken second-hand bookseller, with whom David Copperfield dealt as Mr. Micawber's representative. But neither these sacrifices, nor Mrs. Dickens' abortive efforts at setting up an educational establishment, had been of avail. Her husband's creditors *would not* give him time ; and a dark period began for the family, and more especially for the little eldest son, now ten years old, in which, as he afterwards wrote in bitter anguish of remembrance, " but for the mercy of God, he might easily have become, for any care that was taken of him, a little robber or a little vagabond."

Forster has printed the pathetic fragment of autobiography, communicated to him by Dickens five-and-twenty years after the period to which it refers, and subsequently incorporated with but few changes in the *Personal History of David Copperfield.* Who can forget the thrill with which he first learnt the well-kept secret, that the story of the solitary child, left a prey to the cruel chances of the London streets, was an episode in the life of Charles Dickens himself? Between fact and fiction there was but a difference of names. Murdstone and Grinby's wine warehouse down in Blackfriars, was Jonathan Warren's blacking warehouse at Hungerford Stairs, in which a place had been found for the boy by a relative, a partner in the concern ; and the bottles he had to paste over with labels were in truth blacking-pots. But the menial work and the miserable pay, the uncongenial companionship during worktime, and the speculative devices of the dinner-hour, were the same in each case. At this time, after his family had settled itself in the Marshalsea, the haven open to the little waif at night was a lodging in Little College Street, Camden Town, presenting even fewer attractions than Mr. Micawber's residence in Windsor Terrace, and kept by a lady, afterwards famous under the name of Mrs. Pipchin. His Sundays were spent at home in the prison.

On his urgent remonstrance—"the first I had ever made about my lot"—concerning the distance from his family at which he was left through the week, a back attic was found for him in Lant Street in the Borough, "where Bob Sawyer lodged many years afterwards;" and he now break-fasted and supped with his parents in their apartment. Here they lived in fair comfort, waited upon by a faithful "orfling," who had accompanied the family and its fortunes from Chatham, and who is said by Forster to have her part in the character of the Marchioness. Finally, after the prisoner had obtained his discharge, and had removed with his family to the Lant Street lodgings, a quarrel occurred between the elder Dickens and his cousin, and the boy was in consequence taken away from the business.

He had not been ill-treated there; nor indeed is it ill-treatment which leads to David Copperfield's running away in the story. Nevertheless, it is not strange that Dickens should have looked back with a bitterness very unusual in him, upon the bad old days of his childish soli-tude and degradation. He never "forgot" his mother's having wished him to remain in the warehouse; the subject of his employment there was never afterwards mentioned in the family; he could not bring himself to go near old Hungerford Market so long as it remained standing; and to no human being, not even to his wife, did he speak of this passage in his life, until he narrated it in the fragment of autobiography which he confided to his trusty friend. Such a sensitiveness is not hard to explain; for no man is expected to dilate upon the days "when he lived among the beggars in St. Mary Axe," and it is only the Bounder-bies of society who exult, truly or falsely, in the sordid memories of the time before they became rich or powerful.

And if the sharp experiences of his childhood might have ceased to be resented by one whom the world on the whole treated so kindly, at least they left his heart unhardened, and helped to make him ever tender to the poor and weak, because he too had after a fashion "eaten his bread with tears" when a puny child.

A happy accident having released the David Copperfield of actual life from his unworthy bondage, he was put in the way of an education such as at that time was the lot of most boys of the class to which he belonged. "The world has done much better since in that way, and will do far better yet," he writes at the close of his description of *Our School*, the "Wellington House Academy," situate near that point in the Hampstead Road where modest gentility and commercial enterprise touch hands. Other testimony confirms his sketch of the ignorant and brutal head-master ; and doubtless this worthy and his usher, "considered to know everything as opposed to the chief who was considered to know nothing," furnished some of the features in the portraits of Mr. Creakle and Mr. Mell. But it has been very justly doubted by an old schoolfellow, whether the statement "We were First Boy" is to be regarded as strictly historical. If Charles Dickens, when he entered the school, was "put into Virgil," he was not put there to much purpose. On the other hand, with the return of happier days, had come the resumption of the old amusements which were to grow into the occupations of his life. A club was founded among the boys at Wellington House for the express purpose of circulating short tales written by him, and he was the manager of the private theatricals which they contrived to set on foot.

After two or three years of such work and play it became necessary for Charles Dickens once more to think of earning his bread. His father, who had probably lost his official post at the time when, in Mr. Micawber's phrase, "hope sunk beneath the horizon," was now seeking employment as a parliamentary reporter, and must have rejoiced when a Gray's Inn solicitor of his acquaintance, attracted by the bright clever looks of his son, took the lad into his office as a clerk at a modest weekly salary. His office associates here were perhaps a grade or two above those of the blacking warehouse; but his danger now lay rather in the direction of the vulgarity which he afterwards depicted in such samples of the profession as Mr. Guppy and Mr. Jobling. He is said to have frequented, in company with a fellow-clerk, one of the minor theatres, and even occasionally to have acted there; and assuredly it must have been personal knowledge which suggested the curiously savage description of *Private Theatres* in the *Sketches by Boz*, the all but solitary *unkindly* reference to theatrical amusements in his works. But whatever his experiences of this kind may have been, he passed unscathed through them; and during the year and a half of his clerkship picked up sufficient knowledge of the technicalities of the law to be able to assail its enormities without falling into rudimentary errors about it, and sufficient knowledge of lawyers and lawyers' men to fill a whole chamber in his gallery of characters.

Oddly enough, it was, after all, the example of the father that led the son into the line of life from which he was easily to pass into the career where success and fame awaited him. The elder Dickens having obtained employment as a parliamentary reporter for the *Morning Herald*, his son, who was living with him in Bentinck Street, Manchester Square, resolved to essay the same laborious craft. He was by this time nearly seventeen years of age, and already we notice in

him what were to remain, through life, two of his most
marked characteristics—strength of will, and a determination, if he did a thing at all, to do it thoroughly. The
art of shorthand, which he now resolutely set himself to
master, was in those days no easy study, though, possibly,
in looking back upon his first efforts, David Copperfield
overestimated the difficulties which he had conquered with
the help of love and Traddles. But Dickens, whose education no Dr. Strong had completed, perceived that in order
to succeed as a reporter of the highest class he needed something besides the knowledge of shorthand. In a word,
he lacked reading; and this deficiency he set himself to
supply as best he could by a constant attendance at the
British Museum. Those critics who have dwelt on
the fact that the reading of Dickens was neither very
great nor very extensive, have insisted on what is not
less true than obvious; but he had this one quality
of the true lover of reading, that he never professed a
familiarity with that of which he knew little or nothing.
He continued his visits to the Museum, even when in 1828
he had become a reporter in Doctors' Commons. With
this occupation he had to remain as content as he could
for nearly two years. Once more David Copperfield, the
double of Charles Dickens in his youth, will rise to the
memory of every one of his readers. For not only was his
soul seized with a weariness of Consistory, Arches, Delegates,
and the rest of it, to which he afterwards gave elaborate
expression in his story, but his heart was full of its first
love. In later days, he was not of opinion that he had
loved particularly wisely; but how well he had loved is
known to everyone who after him has lost his heart to Dora.
Nothing came of the fancy, and in course of time he
had composure enough to visit the lady who had been its

object in the company of his wife. He found that Jip was stuffed as well as dead, and that Dora had faded into Flora; for it was as such that, not very chivalrously, he could bring himself to describe her, for the second time, in *Little Dorrit*.

Before at last he was engaged as a reporter on a newspaper, he had, and not for a moment only, thought of turning aside to another profession. It was the profession to which—uncommercially—he was attached during so great a part of his life, that when he afterwards created for himself a stage of his own, he seemed to be but following an irresistible fascination. His best friend described him to me as "a born actor;" and who needs to be told that the world falls into two divisions only—those whose place is before the footlights, and those whose place is behind them? His love of acting was stronger than himself; and I doubt whether he ever saw a play successfully performed without longing to be in and of it. "Assumption," he wrote in after days to Lord Lytton, "has charms for me—I hardly know for how many wild reasons—so delightful that I feel a loss of, oh! I can't say what exquisite foolery, when I lose a chance of being someone in voice, etc. not at all like myself." He loved the theatre and everything which savoured of histrionics with an intensity not even to be imagined by those who have never felt a touch of the same passion. He had that "belief in a play" which he so pleasantly described as one of the characteristics of his lifelong friend, the great painter Clarkson Stanfield. And he had that unextinguishable interest in both actors and acting which makes a little separate world of the "quality." One of the stanchest friendships of his life was that with the foremost English tragedian of his age, Macready; one of the

delights of his last years was his intimacy with another
well-known actor, the late Mr. Fechter. No performer,
however, was so obscure or so feeble as to be outside the
pale of his sympathy. His books teem with kindly likenesses of all manner of entertainers and entertainments—
from Mr. Vincent Crummles and the more or less legitimate drama, down to Mr. Sleary's horse-riding and
Mrs. Jarley's wax-work. He has a friendly feeling
for Chops the dwarf, and for Pickleson the giant;
and in his own quiet Broadstairs he cannot help
tumultuously applauding a young lady "who goes
into the den of ferocious lions, tigers, leopards, etc.
and pretends to go to sleep upon the principal lion, upon
which a rustic keeper, who speaks through his nose,
exclaims: 'Behold the abazid power of woobad!'" He
was unable to sit through a forlorn performance at a
wretched country theatre, without longing to add a sove-
reign to the four and ninepence which he had made out
in the house when he entered, and which "had warmed
up in the course of the evening to twelve shillings;" and
in Bow Street, near his office, he was beset by appeals
such as that of an aged and greasy suitor for an engagement as Pantaloon: "Mr. Dickens, you know our profession, sir—no one knows it better, sir—there is no right
feeling in it. I was Harlequin on your own circuit, sir,
for five-and-thirty years, and was displaced by a boy, sir!
—a boy!" Nor did his disposition change when he
crossed the seas; the streets he first sees in the United
States remind him irresistibly of the set-scene in a London
pantomime; and at Verona his interest is divided between
Romeo and Juliet and the vestiges of an equestrian troupe
in the amphitheatre.

What success Dickens might have achieved as an actor

it is hardly to the present purpose to inquire. A word will be said below of the success he achieved as an amateur actor and manager, and in his more than half dramatic readings. But, the influence of early associations and personal feelings apart, it would seem that the artists of the stage whom he most admired were not those of the highest type. He was subdued by the genius of Frédéric Lemaître, but blind and deaf to that of Ristori. " Sound melodrama and farce " were the dramatic species which he affected, and in which as a professional actor he might have excelled. His intensity might have gone for much in the one, and his versatility and volubility for more in the other ; and in both, as indeed in any kind of play or part, his thoroughness, which extended itself to every detail of performance or make-up, must have stood him in excellent stead. As it was, he was preserved for literature. But he had carefully prepared himself for his intended venture, and when he sought an engagement at Covent Garden, a preliminary interview with the manager was postponed only on account of the illness of the applicant.

Before the next theatrical season opened, he had at last —in the year 1831—obtained employment as a parliamentary reporter, and after some earlier engagements he became, in 1834, one of the reporting staff of the famous Whig *Morning Chronicle,* then in its best days under the editorship of Mr. John Black. Now, for the first time in his life, he had an opportunity of putting forth the energy that was in him. He shrank from none of the difficulties which in those days attended the exercise of his craft. They were thus depicted by himself, when a few years before his death he " held a brief for his brothers" at the dinner of the Newspaper Press Fund : " I have often transcribed for the printer from my shorthand notes important public speeches in which the strictest accuracy was required, and a mistake in which would have been to a young man severely compromising ; writing on the palm of my hand, by the light of a dark lantern, in a post-chaise and four, galloping through a wild country, and through the dead of the night, at the then surprising rate of fifteen miles an hour. . . . I have worn my knees by writing on them on the old back row of the old gallery of the old House of Commons ; and I have worn my feet by standing to write in a preposterous pen in the old House of Lords, where we used to be huddled together like so many sheep kept in waiting, say, until the woolsack might want re-stuffing. Returning home from excited political meetings in the country to the waiting press in London, I do verily believe I have been upset in almost every description of vehicle known in this country. I have been in my time belated on miry by-roads, towards the small hours, forty or fifty miles from London, in a wheelless carriage, with exhausted horses and drunken postboys, and have got back in time for publication, to be received with never-forgotten compliments by the late Mr. Black, coming in the broadest of Scotch from the broadest of hearts I ever knew." Thus early had Dickens learnt the secret of throwing himself into any pursuit once taken up by him, and of half achieving his task by the very heartiness with which he set about it. When at the close of the parliamentary session of the year 1836 his labours as a reporter came to an end, he was held to have no equal in the gallery. During this period his naturally keen powers of observation must have been sharpened and strengthened, and that quickness of decision acquired which constitutes, perhaps, the most valuable lesson that journalistic practice of any kind can teach to a young man of letters. To Dickens' experience as a reporter may likewise be traced no small part of his political creed, in which there was a good deal of infidelity; or at all events, his determined contempt for the parliamentary style proper, whether in the mouth of "Thisman" or of "Thatman," and his rooted dislike of the "cheap-jacks" and "national dustmen" whom he discerned among our orators and legislators. There is probably no very great number of Members of Parliament who are heroes to those who wait attendance on their words. Moreover, the period of Dickens' most active labours as a reporter was one that succeeded a time of great political excitement; and when men wish thankfully to rest after deeds, words are in season.

Meanwhile, very tentatively and with a very imperfect consciousness of the significance for himself of his first steps on a slippery path, Dickens had begun the real career of his life. It has been seen how he had been a writer as a "baby," as a schoolboy, and as a lawyer's clerk, and the time had come when, like all writers, he wished to see himself in print. In December, 1833, the *Monthly Magazine* published a paper which he had dropped into its letter-box, and with eyes "dimmed with joy and pride" the young author beheld his firstborn in print. The paper, called *A Dinner at Poplar Walk*, was afterwards reprinted in the *Sketches by Boz* under the title of *Mr. Minns and his Cousin*, and is laughable enough. His success emboldened him to send further papers of a similar character to the same magazine, which published ten contributions of his by February, 1835. That which appeared in August, 1834, was the first signed "Boz," a nickname given by him in his boyhood to a favourite brother. Since Dickens used this signature not only as the author of the *Sketches* and a few other minor productions, but also as "editor" of the *Pickwick Papers*, it is not surprising that, especially among his admirers on the Continent and in America, the name should have clung to him so tenaciously. It was on a steamboat near Niagara that he heard from his state-room a gentleman complaining to his wife: "Boz keeps himself very close."

But the *Monthly Magazine*, though warmly welcoming its young contributor's lively sketches, could not afford to pay for them. He was therefore glad to conclude an arrangement with Mr. George Hogarth, the conductor of the *Evening Chronicle*, a paper in connexion with the great morning journal on the reporting staff of which he was engaged. He had gratuitously contributed a sketch to the evening paper as a personal favour to Mr. Hogarth, and the latter readily proposed to the proprietors of the *Morning Chronicle* that Dickens should be duly remunerated for this addition to his regular labours. With a salary of seven instead of, as heretofore, five guineas a-week, and settled in chambers in Furnival's Inn—one of those old legal inns which he loved so well—he might already in this year, 1835, consider himself on the high-road to prosperity. By the beginning of 1836 the *Sketches by Boz* printed in the *Evening Chronicle* were already numerous enough, and their success was sufficiently established to allow of his arranging for their republication. They appeared in two volumes, with woodcuts by Cruikshank, and the sum of a hundred and fifty pounds was paid to him for the copyright. The stepping-stones had been found and passed, and on the last day of March, which saw the publication of the first number of the *Pickwick Papers*, he stood in the field of fame

and fortune.   Three days afterwards Dickens married
Catherine Hogarth, the eldest daughter of the friend
who had so efficiently aided him in his early literary
ventures. Mr. George Hogarth's name thus links together
the names of two masters of English fiction; for
Lockhart speaks of him when a Writer to the Signet
in Edinburgh as one of the intimate friends of Scott.
Dickens' apprenticeship as an author was over almost
as soon as it was begun; and he had found the way
short from obscurity to the dazzling light of popularity.
As for the *Sketches by Boz*, their author soon repurchased
the copyright for more than thirteen times the sum which
had been paid to him for it.

In their collected form these *Sketches* modestly described themselves as "illustrative of every-day life and
every-day people."   Herein they only prefigured the more
famous creations of their writer, whose genius was never
so happy as when lighting up, now the humorous, now
what he chose to term the romantic side of familiar
things.   The curious will find little difficulty in tracing
in these outlines, often rough and at times coarse, the
groundwork of more than one finished picture of later
date.   Not a few of the most peculiar features of Dickens
humour are already here, together with not a little of his
most characteristic pathos.   It is true that in these early
Sketches the latter is at times strained, but its power is
occasionally beyond denial, as, for instance, in the brief
narrative of the death of the hospital patient.   On the
other hand, the humour—more especially that of the
Tales—is not of the most refined sort, and often de-
generates in the direction of boisterous farce.   The style,
too, though in general devoid of the pretentiousness
which is the bane of "light" journalistic writing, has

ᴄ

a taint of vulgarity about it, very pardonable under the circumstances, but generally absent from Dickens' later works. Weak puns are not unfrequent; and the diction but rarely reaches that exquisite felicity of comic phrase in which *Pickwick* and its successors excel. For the rest, Dickens' favourite passions and favourite aversions alike reflect themselves here in small. In the description of the Election for Beadle he ridicules the tricks and the manners of political party-life, and his love of things theatrical has its full freshness upon it,— however he may pretend at Astley's that his "histrionic taste is gone," and that it is the audience which chiefly delights him. But of course the gift which these *Sketches* pre-eminently revealed in their author was a descriptive power that seemed to lose sight of nothing characteristic in the object described, and of nothing humorous in an association suggested by it. Whether his theme was street or river, a Christmas dinner or the extensive groves of the illustrious dead (the old clothes' shops in Monmouth Street), he reproduced it in all its shades and colours, and under a hundred aspects, fanciful as well as real. How inimitable, for instance, is the sketch of "the last cab-driver, and the first omnibus cad," whose earlier vehicle, the omnipresent "red cab," was not the gondola, but the very fire-ship of the London streets.

Dickens himself entertained no high opinion of these youthful efforts; and in this he showed the consciousness of the true artist, that masterpieces are rarely thrown off at hazard. But though much of the popularity of the *Sketches* may be accounted for by the fact that common-place people love to read about commonplace people and things, the greater part of it is due to genuine literary merit. The days of half-price in theatres have followed the days of coaching; "Honest Tom" no more paces the lobby in a black coat with velvet facings and cuffs, and a D'Orsay hat; the Hickses of the present time no longer quote "Don Juan" over boarding-house dinner-tables; and the young ladies in Camberwell no longer compare young men in attitudes to Lord Byron, or to "Satan" Montgomery. But the *Sketches by Boz* have survived their birth-time; and they deserve to be remembered among the rare instances in which a young author has no sooner begun to write, than he has shown a knowledge of his real strength. As yet, however, this sudden favourite of the public was unaware of the range to which his powers were to extend, and of the height to which they were to mount.

CHAPTER II.

1836—1841.

EVEN in those years of which the record is brightest in the story of his life, Charles Dickens, like the rest of the world, had his share of troubles—troubles great and small, losses which went home to his heart, and vexations manifold in the way of business. But in the history of his early career as an author, the word failure has no place.

Not that the *Posthumous Papers of the Pickwick Club*, published as they were in monthly numbers, at once took the town by storm; for the public needed two or three months to make up its mind that "Boz" was equal to an effort considerably in advance of his *Sketches*. But when the popularity of the serial was once established, it grew with extraordinary rapidity until it reached an altogether unprecedented height. He would be a bold man who should declare that its popularity has very materially diminished at the present day. Against the seductions of *Pickwick* and of other works of amusement of which it was the prototype, Dr. Arnold thought himself bound seriously to contend among the boys of Rugby; and twenty years later young men at the university talked nothing but *Pickwick*, and quoted nothing but *Pickwick*, and the wittiest of undergraduates set the world at large an examination paper in *Pickwick*, over which pretentious half-knowledge may puzzle, unable accurately to "describe the common Profeel-machine," or to furnish a satisfactory definition of "a red-faced Nixon." No changes in manners and customs have interfered with the hold of the work upon nearly all classes of readers at home; and no translation has been dull enough to prevent its being relished even in countries where all English manners and customs must seem equally uninteresting or equally absurd.

So extraordinary has been the popularity of this more than thrice fortunate book, that the wildest legends have grown up as to the history of its origin. The facts, however, as stated by Dickens himself, are few and plain. Attracted by the success of the *Sketches*, Messrs. Chapman and Hall proposed to him that he should write "something" in monthly numbers to serve as a vehicle for certain plates to be executed by the comic draughtsman, Mr. R. Seymour; and either the publishers or the artist suggested as a kind of leading notion, the idea of a "Nimrod Club" of unlucky sportsmen. The proposition was at Dickens' suggestion so modified that the plates were "to arise naturally out of the text," the range of the latter being left open to him. This explains why the rather artificial machinery of a club was maintained, and why Mr. Winkle's misfortunes by flood and field hold their place by the side of the philanthropical meanderings of Mr. Pickwick and the amorous experiences of Mr. Tupman. An original was speedily found for the pictorial presentment of the hero of the book, and a felicitous name for him soon suggested itself. Only a single number of the serial had appeared when Mr. Seymour's own hand put an end to his life. It is well known that among the applicants for the vacant office of illustrator of the *Pickwick*

which the book was begun and carried on make it preposterous to judge it by canons applicable to its author's
subsequent fictions.   As the serial proceeded, the interest
which was to be divided between the inserted tales,
some of which have real merit, and the framework, was
absorbed by the latter.   The rise in the style of the book
can almost be measured by the change in the treatment
of its chief character, Mr. Pickwick himself.   In a later
preface, Dickens endeavoured to illustrate this change by
the analogy of real life.   The truth of course is, that it
was only as the author proceeded that he recognised the
capabilities of the character, and his own power of
making it, and his book with it, truly loveable as well
as laughable.   Thus, on the very same page in which
Mr. Pickwick proves himself a true gentleman in his
leave-taking from Mr. Nupkins, there follows a little
bit of the idyll between Sam and the pretty house-
maid, written with a delicacy that could hardly have
been suspected in the chronicler of the experiences of
Miss Jemima Evans or of Mr. Augustus Cooper.   In the
subsequent part of the main narrative will be found
exemplified nearly all the varieties of pathos of which
Dickens was afterwards so repeatedly to prove himself
master, more especially of course in those prison scenes
for which some of our older novelists may have furnished
him with hints.   Even that subtle species of humour is
not wanting which is content to miss its effect with the
less attentive reader; as in this passage concerning the
ruined cobbler's confidences to Sam in the Fleet :

The cobbler paused to ascertain what effect his story had produced on Sam; but finding that he had dropped asleep, knocked
the ashes out of his pipe, *sighed*, put it down, drew the bedclothes
over his head, and went to sleep too.

Goldsmith himself could not have put more of pathos and more of irony into a single word.

But it may seem out of place to dwell upon details such as this in view of the broad and universally acknowledged comic effects of this masterpiece of English humour. Its many genuinely comic characters are as broadly marked as the heroes of the least refined of sporting novels, and as true to nature as the most elaborated products of Addison's art. The author's humour is certainly not one which eschews simple in favour of subtle means, or which is averse from occasional desipience in the form of the wildest farce. Mrs. Leo Hunter's garden party—or rather "public break-fast"—at The Den, Eatanswill; Mr. Pickwick's nocturnal descent, through three gooseberry bushes and a rose-tree, upon the virgin soil of Miss Tomkins' establishment for young ladies; the *supplice d'un homme* of Mr. Pott; Mr. Weller junior's love-letter, with notes and comments by Mr. Weller senior, and Mr. Weller senior's own letter of affliction written by somebody else; the footmen's "swarry" at Bath, and Mr. Bob Sawyer's bachelors' party in the Borough;—all these and many other scenes and passages have in them that jovial element of exaggeration which nobody mistakes and nobody resents. Whose duty is it to check the volubility of Mr. Alfred Jingle, or to weigh the heaviness, *quot libras*, of the Fat Boy? Every-one is conscious of the fact that in the contagious high spirits of the author lies one of the chief charms of the book. Not, however, that the effect produced is obtained without the assistance of a very vigilant art. Nowhere is this more apparent than in the character which is upon the whole the most brilliant of the many brilliant additions which the author made to his original group of personages. If there is nothing so humorous in the book as Sam Weller, neither is there in it anything more pathetic than the relation between him and his master. As for Sam Weller's style of speech, scant justice was done to it by Mr. Pickwick when he observed to Job Trotter, "my man is in the right, although his mode of expressing his opinion is somewhat homely, and occasionally incomprehensible." The fashion of Sam's gnomic philosophy is at least as old as Theocritus;[1] but the special impress which he has given to it is his own, rudely foreshadowed perhaps in some of the apophthegms of his father. Incidental Sam Wellerisms in *Oliver Twist* and *Nicholas Nickleby* show how enduring a hold the whimsical fancy had taken of its creator. For the rest, the freshness of the book continues the same to the end; and farcical as are some of the closing scenes—those, for instance, in which a chorus of coachmen attends the movements of the elder Mr. Weller—there is even here no straining after effect. An exception might perhaps be found in the catastrophe of the Shepherd, which is coarsely contrived; but the fun of the character is in itself neither illegitimate nor unwholesome. It will be observed below that it is the constant harping on the same string, the repeated picturing of professional preachers of religion as gross and greasy scoundrels, which in the end becomes offensive in Dickens.

On the whole, no hero has ever more appropriately bidden farewell to his labours than Mr. Pickwick in the words which he uttered at the table of the ever-hospitable Mr. Wardle at the Adelphi.

---

[1] See *Idyll.* xv. 77. This discovery is not my own, but that of the late Dr. Donaldson, who used to translate the passage accordingly with great gusto.

"I shall never regret," said Mr. Pickwick in a low voice, "I shall never regret having devoted the greater part of two years to mixing with different varieties and shades of human character; frivolous as my pursuit of novelty may appear to many. Nearly the whole of my previous life having been devoted to business and the pursuit of wealth, numerous scenes of which I had no previous conception have dawned upon me—I hope to the enlargement of my mind, and to the improvement of my understanding. If I have done but little good, I trust I have done less harm, and that none of my adventures will be other than a source of amusing and pleasant recollection to me in the decline of life. God bless you all."

Of course Mr. Pickwick "filled and drained a bumper" to the sentiment. Indeed, it "snoweth" in this book "of meat and drink." Wine, ale, and brandy abound there, and viands to which ample justice is invariably done— even under Mr. Tupman's heartrending circumstances at the (now, alas! degenerate) Leather Bottle. Something of this is due to the times in which the work was composed, and to the class of readers for which we may suppose it in the first instance to have been intended; but Dickens, though a temperate man, loved the paraphernalia of good cheer, besides cherishing the associations which are inseparable from it. At the same time, there is a little too much of it in the *Pickwick Papers*, however well its presence may consort with the geniality which pervades them. It is difficult to turn any page of the book without chancing on one of those supremely felicitous phrases in the ready mintage of which Dickens at all times excelled. But its chief attraction lies in the spirit of the whole— that spirit of true humour, which calls forth at once merriment, good will, and charity.

In the year 1836, which the commencement of the *Pickwick Papers* has made memorable in the history of English literature, Dickens was already in the full tide of authorship. In February, 1837, the second number of *Bentley's Miscellany*, a new monthly magazine which he had undertaken to edit, contained the opening chapters of his story of *Oliver Twist*. Shortly before this, in September and December, 1836, he had essayed two of the least ambitious branches of dramatic authorship. The acting of Harley, an admirable dry comedian, gave some vitality to *Thè Strange Gentleman*, a "comic bur-letta," or farce, in two acts, founded upon the tale in the *Sketches* called *The Great Winglebury Duel*. It ran for seventy nights at Drury Lane, and, in its author's opinion, was "the best thing Harley did." But the adaptation has no special feature distinguishing it from the original, unless it be the effective bustle of the opening. *The Village Coquettes*, an operetta represented at the St. James's Theatre, with music by Hullah, was an equally unpretending effort. In this piece Harley took one part, that of "a very small farmer with a very large circle of intimate friends," and John Parry made his *début* on the London stage in another. To quote any of the songs in this operetta would be very unfair to Dickens.[1] He was not at all depressed by the unfavourable criticisms which were passed upon his libretto, and against which he had to set the round declaration of Braham, that there had been "no such music since the days of Shield, and no such piece since *The Duenna*." As time went on, however, he became anything but proud of his juvenile productions as a dramatist, and strongly objected to their revival. His third and last attempt of this kind,

[1] For operas, as a form of *dramatic* entertainment, Dickens seems afterwards to have entertained a strong contempt, such as, indeed, it is difficult for any man with a sense of humour wholly to avoid.

a farce called *The Lamplighter*, which he wrote for Covent
Garden in 1838, was never acted, having been withdrawn
by Macready's wish; and in 1841 Dickens converted it
into a story printed among the *Pic-Nic Papers*, a collection
generously edited by him for the benefit of the widow
and children of a publisher towards whom he had little
cause for personal gratitude.   His friendship for Macready
kept alive in him for some time the desire to write a
comedy worthy of so distinguished an actor; and, according to his wont, he had even chosen beforehand for the
piece a name which he was not to forget—*No Thoroughfare*.   But the genius of the age, an influence which is
often stronger than personal wishes or inclinations,
diverted him from dramatic composition.   He would
have been equally unwilling to see mentioned among
his literary works the *Life of Grimaldi*, which he merely
edited, and which must be numbered among forgotten
memorials of forgotten greatness.

To the earlier part of 1838 belong one or two other
publications, which their author never cared to reprint.
The first of these, however, a short pamphlet entitled
Sunday under Three Heads, is not without a certain
biographical interest.   This little book was written with
immediate reference to a bill "for the better observance of
the Sabbath," which the House of Commons had recently
thrown out by a small majority; and its special purpose
was the advocacy of Sunday excursions, and harmless
Sunday amusements, in lieu of the alternate gloom
and drunkenness distinguishing what Dickens called a
London *Sunday as it is*.   His own love of fresh air and
brightness intensified his hatred of a formalism which
shuts its ears to argument.   In the powerful picture of a
Sunday evening in London, "gloomy, close, and stale,"

which he afterwards drew in *Little Dorrit*, he almost seems to hold Sabbatarianism and the weather responsible for one another.   When he afterwards saw a Parisian Sunday, he thought it "not comfortable," so that, like others who hate bigotry, he may perhaps have come to recognise the difficulty of arranging an English *Sunday as it might be made*.   On the other hand, he may have remembered his youthful fancy of the good clergyman encouraging a game of cricket after church, when thirty years later, writing from Edinburgh, he playfully pictured the counterpart of *Sunday as Sabbath bills would have it* : describing how "the usual preparations are making for the band in the open air in the afternoon, and the usual pretty children (selected for that purpose), are at this moment hanging garlands round the Scott monument preparatory to the innocent Sunday dance round that edifice, with which the diversions invariably close." The *Sketches of Young Gentlemen*, published in the same year, are little if at all in advance of the earlier *Sketches by Boz*, and were evidently written to order. He finished them in precisely a fortnight, and noted in his diary that " one hundred and twenty-five pounds for such a book, without any name to it, is pretty well." The *Sketches of Young Couples*, which followed as late as 1840, have the advantage of a facetious introduction, suggested by Her Majesty's own announcement of her approaching marriage.   But the life has long gone out of these pleasantries, as it has from others of the same cast, in which many a mirthful spirit, forced to coin its mirth into money, has ere now spent itself.

It was the better fortune of Dickens to be able almost from the first to keep nearly all his writings on a level with his powers.   He never made a bolder step forwards

than when, in the very midst of the production of *Pickwick*,
he began his first long continuous story, the *Adventures
of Oliver Twist*. Those who have looked at the MS. of
this famous novel will remember the vigour of the handwriting, and how few, in comparison with his later MSS.,
are the additions and obliterations which it exhibits.
But here and there the writing shows traces of excitement; for the author's heart was in his work, and
much of it, contrary to his later habit, was written at
night. No doubt he was upheld in the labour of authorship by something besides ambition and consciousness of
strength. *Oliver Twist* was certainly written *with a
purpose*, and with one that was afterwards avowed. The
author intended to put before his readers—" so long as
their speech did not offend the ear "—a picture of " dregs
of life," hitherto, as he believed, never exhibited by any
novelist in their loathsome reality. Yet the old masters
of fiction, Fielding in particular, as well as the old master
of the brush whom Dickens cites (Hogarth), had not
shrunk from the path which their disciple now essayed.
Dickens, however, was naturally thinking of his own
generation, which had already relished *Paul Clifford*, and
which was not to be debarred from exciting itself over
Jack Sheppard, begun before *Oliver Twist* had been completed, and in the selfsame magazine. Dickens' purpose
was an honest and a praiseworthy one. But the most
powerful and at the same time the most loveable element
in his genius suggested the silver lining to the cloud.
To that unfailing power of sympathy which was the main-
spring of both his most affecting and his most humorous
touches, we owe the redeeming features in his company of
criminals ; not only the devotion and the heroism of
Nancy, but the irresistible vivacity of the Artful Dodger,

and the good-humour of Charley Bates, which moved
Talfourd to "plead as earnestly in mitigation of judgment"
against him as ever he had done "at the bar for any client
he most respected." Other parts of the story were less
carefully tempered. Mr. Fang, the police-magistrate, appears to have been a rather hasty portrait of a living original;
and the whole picture of Bumble and Bumbledom was
certainly a caricature of the working of the new Poor-
Law, confounding the question of its merits and demerits
with that of its occasional maladministration. On the
other hand, a vein of truest pathos runs through the whole
of poor Nancy's story, and adds to the effect of a marvel-
lously powerful catastrophe. From Nancy's interview
with Rose at London Bridge to the closing scenes, the
flight of Sikes, his death at Jacob's Island, and the end of
the Jew, the action has an intensity rare in the literature
of the terrible. By the side of this genuine tragic force,
which perhaps it would be easiest to parallel from some
of the "low" domestic tragedy of the Elizabethans, the
author's comic humour burst forth upon the world in a
variety of entirely new types: Bumble and his partner;
Noah Claypole, complete in himself, but full of promise
for Uriah Heep; and the Jew, with all the pupils and
supporters of his establishment of technical education.
Undeniably the story of *Oliver Twist* also contains much
that is artificial and stilted, with much that is weak
and (the author of *Endymion* is to be thanked for
the word) "gushy." Thus, all the Maylie scenes, down
to the last in which Oliver discreetly "glides" away
from the lovers, are barely endurable. But, whatever its
shortcomings, *Oliver Twist* remains an almost unique
example of a young author's brilliant success in an
enterprise of complete novelty and extreme difficulty.

the present. Dickens was never so strong as when he produced from the real; and in this instance,—starting, no doubt, with a healthy prejudice,—so carefully had he inspected the neighbourhood of the Yorkshire schools, of which Dotheboys Hall was to be held up as the infamous type, that there seems to be no difficulty in identifying the site of the very school itself; while the Portsmouth Theatre is to the full as accurate a study as the Yorkshire school. So, again, as everyone knows, the Brothers Cheeryble were real personages well known in Manchester,[1] where even the original of Tim Linkinwater still survives in local remembrance. On the other hand, with how conscious a strength has the author's imaginative power used and transmuted his materials: in the Squeers family, creating a group of inimitable grotesqueness; in their humblest victim Smike giving one of his earliest pictures of those outcasts whom he drew again and again with such infinite tenderness; and in Mr. Vincent Crummles and his company, including the Phenomenon, establishing a jest, but a kindly one, for all times! In a third series of episodes in this book, it is universally agreed that the author has no less conspicuously failed. Dickens' first attempt to picture the manners and customs of the aristocracy certainly resulted in portraying some very peculiar people. Lord Frederick Verisopht, indeed— who is allowed to redeem his character in the end—is not without touches resembling nature.

"I take an interest, my lord," said Mrs. Wititterly, with a faint smile; "such an interest in the drama."

"Ye-es. It's very interasting," replied Lord Frederick.

"I'm always ill after Shakespeare," said Mrs. Wititterly, "I

---

[1] W. and D. Grant Brothers had their warehouse at the lower end of Cannon Street, and their private house in Mosely Street.

scarcely exist the next day; I find the reaction so very great after a tragedy, my lord, and Shakespeare is such a delicious creature."

"Ye-es!" replied Lord Frederick. "He was a clayver man."

But Sir Mulberry Hawk is a kind of scoundrel not frequently met with in polite society; his henchmen Pluck and Pyke have the air of "followers of Don John," and the enjoyments of the "trainers of young noblemen and gentlemen" at Hampton races, together with the riotous debauch which precedes the catastrophe, seem taken direct from the transpontine stage. The fact is that Dickens was here content to draw his vile seducers and wicked orgies, just as commonplace writers had drawn them a thousand times before, and will draw them a thousand times again. Much of the hero's talk is of the same conventional kind. On the other hand, nothing could be more genuine than the flow of fun in this book, which finds its outlet in the most unexpected channels, but nowhere so resistlessly as in the invertebrate talk of Mrs. Nickleby. For her Forster discovered a literary prototype in a character of Miss Austen's; but even if Mrs. Nickleby was founded on Miss Bates, in *Emma*, she left her original far behind. Miss Bates, indeed, is verbose, roundabout, and parenthetic; but the widow never deviates into coherence.

Nicholas Nickleby shows the comic genius of its author in full activity, and should be read with something of the buoyancy of spirit in which it was written, and not with a callousness capable of seeing in so amusing a scamp as Mr. Mantalini one of Dickens' "monstrous failures." At the same time this book displays the desire of the author to mould his manner on the old models. The very title has a savour of Smollett about it; the style has more than one reminiscence of him, as well as of Fielding and of Goldsmith ; and the general method of the narrative resembles that of our old novelists and their Spanish and French predecessors. Partly for this reason, and partly, no doubt, because of the rapidity with which the story was written, its construction is weaker than is usual even with Dickens' earlier works. Coincidences are repeatedly employed to help on the action ; and the *dénoûment*, which, besides turning Mr. Squeers into a thief, reveals Ralph Nickleby as the father of Smike, is oppressively complete. As to the practical aim of the novel, the author's word must be taken for the fact that " Mr. Squeers and his school were faint and feeble pictures of an existing reality, purposely subdued and kept down lest they should be deemed impossible." The exposure, no doubt, did good in its way, though perhaps Mr. Squeers, in a more or less modified form, has proved a tougher adversary to overcome than Mrs. Gamp.

During these years Dickens was chiefly resident in the modest locality of Doughty Street, whither he had moved his household from the " three rooms," " three storeys high," in Furnival's Inn, early in 1837. It was not till the end of 1839 that he took up his abode, further west, in a house which he came to like best among all his London habitations, in Devonshire Terrace, Regent's Park. His town life was, however, varied by long rustications at Twickenham and at Petersham, and by sojourns at the sea-side, of which he was a most consistent votary. He is found in various years of his life at Brighton, Dover, and Bonchurch—where he liked his neighbours better than he liked the climate ; and in later years, when he had grown accustomed to the Continent, he repeatedly do-mesticated himself at Boulogne. But already in 1837 he had discovered the little seaside village, as it then

was, which for many years afterwards became his
favourite holiday retreat, and of which he would be the
genius loci, even if he had not by a special description
immortalised *Our English Watering-place*. Broadstairs—
whose afternoon tranquillity even to this day is undis-
turbed except by the Ethiopians on their tramp from
Margate to Ramsgate—and its constant visitor, are thus
described in a letter written to an American friend in 1843 :
"This is a little fishing-place ; intensely quiet ; built
on a cliff, whereon—in the centre of a tiny semicircular
bay—our house stands ; the sea rolling and dashing under
the windows. Seven miles out are the Goodwin Sands
(you've heard of the Goodwin Sands ?) whence floating
lights perpetually wink after dark, as if they were
carrying on intrigues with the servants. Also there is a
big lighthouse called the North Foreland on a hill behind
the village, a severe parsonic light, which reproves the
young and giddy floaters, and stares grimly out upon the
sea. Under the cliff are rare good sands, where all the
children assemble every morning and throw up impossible
fortifications, which the sea throws down again at high
water. Old gentlemen and ancient ladies flirt after their
own manner in two reading-rooms and on a great many
scattered seats in the open air. Other old gentlemen look
all day through telescopes and never see anything. In a
bay-window in a one-pair sits, from nine o'clock to one, a
gentleman with rather long hair and no neckcloth, who
writes and grins, as if he thought he were very funny
indeed. His name is Boz."

Not a few houses at Broadstairs may boast of having
been at one time or another inhabited by him and his.
Of the long-desired Fort House, however, which local
perverseness triumphantly points out as the original of

Bleak House (no part even of *Bleak House* was written there, though part of *David Copperfield* was), he could not obtain possession till 1850. As like Bleak House as it is like Chesney Wold, it stands at the very highest end of the place, looking straight out to sea, over the little harbour and its two colliers, with a pleasant stretch of cornfields leading along the cliff towards the lighthouse which Dickens promised Lord Carlisle should serve him as a night-light. But in 1837 Dickens was content with narrower quarters. The "long small procession of sons" and daughters had as yet only begun with the birth of his eldest boy. His life was simple and full of work, and occasional seaside or country quarters, and now and then a brief holiday tour, afforded the necessary refreshment of change. In 1837 he made his first short trip abroad, and in the following year, accompanied by Mr. Hablot Browne, he spent a week of enjoyment in Warwickshire, noting in his *Remembrancer:* "Stratford; Shakespeare; the birth-place; visitors, scribblers, old woman (query whether she knows what Shakespeare did), etc." Meanwhile, among his truest home enjoyments were his friendships. They were few in number, mostly with men for whom, after he had once taken them into his heart, he preserved a lifelong regard. Chief of all these were John Forster and Daniel Maclise, the high-minded painter, to whom we owe a charming portrait of his friend in this youthful period of his life. Losing them, he afterwards wrote when absent from England, was "like losing my arms and legs, and dull and tame I am without you." Besides these, he was at this time on very friendly terms with William Harrison Ainsworth, who succeeded him in the editorship of the *Miscellany*, and concerning whom he exclaimed in his *Remembrancer:* "Ainsworth has a fine heart." At the

close of 1838, Dickens, Ainsworth, and Forster constituted
themselves a club called the Trio, and afterwards the
Cerberus. Another name frequent in the *Remembrancer*
entries is that of Talfourd, a generous friend, in whom, as
Dickens finely said after his death, " the success of other
men made as little change as his own." All these, together
with Stanfield, the Landseers, Douglas Jerrold, Macready,
and others less known to fame, were among the friends
and associates of Dickens' prime. The letters, too, remain-
ing from this part of Dickens' life, have all the same
tone of unaffected frankness. With some of his intimate
friends he had his established epistolary jokes. Stanfield, the great marine painter, he pertinaciously treated
as a "very salt" correspondent, communications to
whom, as to a "block-reeving, main-brace-splicing, lead-
heaving, ship-conning, stun'sail-bending, deck-swabbing
son of a sea-cook," needed garnishing with the obscurest
technicalities and strangest oaths of his element. (It is
touching to turn from these friendly buffooneries to a
letter written by Dickens many years afterwards—in 1867
—and mentioning a visit to " poor dear Stanfield," when
" it was clear that the shadow of the end had fallen on
him. . . . It happened well that I had seen, on a wild day
at Tynemouth, a remarkable sea effect, of which I wrote a
description to him, and he had kept it under his pillow.")
Macready, after his retirement from the stage, is bantered
on the score of his juvenility with a pertinacity of fun
recalling similar whimsicalities of Charles Lamb's; or the
jest is changed, and the great London actor in his rural
retreat is depicted in the character of a country gentleman
strange to the wicked ways of the town. As in the case
of many delightful letter-writers, the charm of Dickens
as a correspondent vanishes so soon as he becomes self-

conscious. Even in his letters to Lady Blessington and
Mrs. Watson, a striving after effect is at times perceptible ;
the homage rendered to Lord John Russell is not offered
with a light hand ; on the contrary, when writing to
Douglas Jerrold, Dickens is occasionally so intent upon
proving himself a sound Radical that his vehemence all
but passes into a shriek.

In these early years, at all events, Dickens was happy
in the society of his chosen friends. His favourite amusements were a country walk or ride with Forster, or a
dinner at Jack Straw's Castle with him and Maclise.
He was likewise happy at home. Here, however, in
the very innermost circle of his affections, he had to
suffer the first great personal grief of his life. His
younger sister-in-law, Miss Mary Hogarth, had accompanied him and his wife into their new abode in
Doughty Street, and here, in May, 1837, she died, at
the early age of seventeen. No sorrow seems ever to have
touched the heart and possessed the imagination of Charles
Dickens like that for the loss of this dearly-loved girl,
" young, beautiful, and good." " I can solemnly say," he
wrote to her mother a few months after her death, " that,
waking or sleeping, I have never lost the recollection of
our hard trial and sorrow, and I feel that I never shall."
" If," ran part of his first entry in the Diary which he
began on the first day of the following year, " she were
with us now, the same winning, happy, amiable companion, sympathising with all my thoughts and feelings
more than anyone I knew ever did or will, I think I
should have nothing to wish for but a continuance of such
happiness. But she is gone, and pray God I may one day,
through His mercy, rejoin her." It was not till, in after
years, it became necessary to abandon the project, that he

ceased to cherish the intention of being buried by her side, and through life the memory of her haunted him with strange vividness. At the Niagara Falls, when the spectacle of Nature in her glory had produced in him, as he describes it, a wondrously tranquil and happy peace of mind, he longed for the presence of his dearest friends, and "I was going to add, what would I give if the dear girl, whose ashes lie in Kensal Green, had lived to come so far along with us; but she has been here many times, I doubt not, since her sweet face faded from my earthly sight." "After she died," he wrote to her mother in May, 1843, "I dreamed of her every night for many weeks, and always with a kind of quiet happiness, which became so pleasant to me that I never lay down at night without a hope of the vision coming back in one shape or other. And so it did." Once he dreamt of her, when travelling in Yorkshire; and then, after an interval of many months, as he lay asleep one night at Genoa, it seemed to him as if her spirit visited him and spoke to him in words which he afterwards precisely remembered, when he had awaked, with the tears running down his face. He never forgot her, and in the year before he died, he wrote to his friend : "She is so much in my thoughts at all times, especially when I am successful, and have greatly prospered in anything, that the recollection of her is an essential part of my being, and is as inseparable from my existence as the beating of my heart is!" In a word, she was the object of the one great imaginative passion of his life. Many have denied that there is any likeness to nature in the fictitious figure in which, according to the wont of imaginative workers, he was irresistibly impelled to embody the sentiment with which she inspired him; but the sentiment itself became part of his nature, and part of his history.

When in writing the *Old Curiosity Shop* he approached
the death of Little Nell, he shrank from the task. " Dear
Mary died yesterday, when I think of this sad story."

The *Old Curiosity Shop* has long been freed from the
encumbrances which originally surrounded it, and there
is little except biographical interest in the half-forgotten
history of *Master Humphrey's Clock*. Early in the year
1840, his success and confidence in his powers induced him
to undertake an illustrated weekly journal, in which he
depended solely on his own name, and, in the first instance,
on his own efforts, as a writer. Such was his trust in his
versatility, that he did not think it necessary even to open
with a continuous story. Perhaps the popularity of the
Pickwick Papers encouraged him to adopt the time-honoured
device of wrapping up several tales in one. In any case,
his framework was in the present instance too elaborate to
take hold of the public mind, while the characters introduced
into it possessed little or nothing of the freshness of their
models in the *Tatler* and the *Spectator*. In order to
reinforce Master Humphrey, the deaf gentleman, and the
other original members of his benevolent conclave, he
hereupon resorted to a natural, but none the less unhappy,
expedient. Mr. Pickwick was revived, together with
Sam Weller and his parent ; and a Weller of the third
generation was brought on the stage in the person of
a precocious four-year-old, " standing with his little legs
very wide apart as if the top-boots were familiar to
them, and actually winking upon the housekeeper with
his infant eye, in imitation of his grandfather." A
laugh may have been raised at the time by this attempt,
from which, however, every true Pickwickian must have
turned sadly away. Nor was there much in the other
contents of these early numbers to make up for the dis-

measure out of themselves, will be likely to tire of the conception, or to declare its execution artificial.   Curiously enough, not only was Little Nell a favourite of Landor, a poet and critic utterly averse from meretricious art, but she also deeply moved the sympathy of Lord Jeffrey, who at least knew his own mind, and spoke it in both praise and blame.   As already stated, Dickens only with difficulty brought himself to carry his story to its actual issue, though it is hard to believe that he could ever have intended a different close from that which he gave to it.   His whole heart was in the story, nor could he have consoled himself by means of an ordinary happy ending.

Dickens' comic humour never flowed in a pleasanter vein than in the *Old Curiosity Shop*, and nowhere has it a more exquisite element of pathos in it.   The shock-headed, red-cheeked Kit is one of the earliest of those ungainly figures who speedily find their way into our affections— the odd family to which Mr. Toots, Tom Pinch, Tommy Traddles, and Joe Gargery alike belong.   But the triumph of this serio-comic form of art in the *Old Curiosity Shop* is to be found in the later experiences of Dick Swiveller, who seems at first merely a more engaging sample of the Bob Sawyer species, but who ends by endearing himself to the most thoughtless laugher.   Dick Swiveller and his protegee have gained a lasting place among the favourite characters of English fiction, and the privations of the Marchioness have possibly had a result which would have been that most coveted by Dickens—that of helping towards the better treatment of a class whose lot is among the dust and ashes, too often very bitter ashes, of many households. Besides these, the story contains a variety of incidental characters of a class which Dickens never grew weary of drawing from the life.   Messrs. Codlin, Short, and little demon is so blended with his surroundings—the description of which forms one of the author's most telling pictures of the lonely foulnesses of the riverside, —that his life seems natural in its way, and his death a most appropriate ending to it. Sally Brass, "whose accomplishments were all of a masculine and strictly legal kind," is less of a caricature, and not without a humorously redeeming point of feminine weakness; yet the end of her and her brother is described at the close of the book with almost tragic earnestness. On the whole, though the poetic sympathy of Dickens when he wrote this book was absorbed in the character of his heroine, yet his genius rarely asserted itself after a more diversified fashion.

Of *Barnaby Rudge*, though in my opinion an excellent book after its kind, I may speak more briefly. With the exception of *A Tale of Two Cities*, it was Dickens' only attempt in the historical novel. In the earlier work the relation between the foreground and background of the story is skilfully contrived, and the colouring of the whole, without any elaborate attempt at accurate fidelity, has a generally true and harmonious effect. With the help of her portrait by a painter (Mr. Frith) for whose pictures Dickens had a great liking, Dolly Varden has justly taken hold of the popular fancy as a charming type of a pretty girl of a century ago. And some of the local descriptions in the early part of the book are hardly less pleasing: the Temple in summer, as it was before the charm of Fountain Court was destroyed by its guardians; and the picturesque comforts of the Maypole Inn, described beforehand, by way of contrast to the desecration of its central sanctuary. The intrigue of the story is fairly interesting in itself, and the gentlemanly villain who plays a principal part in it, though, as usual, over-elaborated, is drawn with more skill than Dickens usually displays in such characters. After the main interest of the book has passed to the historical action of the George Gordon riots, the story still retains its coherence, and, a few minor improbabilities apart, is successfully conducted to its close. No historical novel can altogether avoid the banalities of the species; and though Dickens, like all the world, had his laugh at the late Mr. G. P. R. James, he is constrained to introduce the historical hero of the tale, with his confidential adviser, and his attendant, in the familiar guise of three horsemen. As for Lord George Gordon himself, and the riots of which the responsibility remains inseparable from his unhappy memory, the representation of them in the novel sufficiently accords both with poetic probability and with historical fact. The poor lord's evil genius indeed, Gashford—who has no historical original—tries the reader's sense of verisimilitude rather hard; such converts are uncommon except among approvers. The Protestant hangman, on the other hand, has some slight historical warranty; but the leading part which he is made to play in the riots, and his resolution to go any lengths "in support of the great Protestant principle of hanging," overshoot the mark. It cannot be said that there is any substantial exaggeration in the description of the riots; thus, the burning of the great distiller's house in Holborn is a well-authenticated fact; and there is abundant vigour in the narrative. Repetition is unavoidable in treating such a theme, but in *Barnaby Rudge* it is not rendered less endurable by mannerism, nor puffed out with rhetoric.

One very famous character in this story was, as personages in historical novels often are, made up out of two originals.[1] This was Grip the Raven, who, after seeing the idiot hero of the tale safe through his adventures, resumed his addresses on the subject of the kettle to the horses in the stable; and who, " as he was a mere infant when Barnaby was gray, has very probably gone on talking to the present time." In a later preface to *Barnaby Rudge*, Dickens, with infinite humour, related his experiences of the two originals in question, and how he had been ravenless since the mournful death before the kitchen fire of the second of the pair, the *Grip* of actual life. This occurred in the house at Devonshire Terrace, into which the family had moved two years before (in 1839).

As Dickens' fame advanced, his circle of acquaintances was necessarily widened; and in 1841 he was invited to visit Edinburgh, and to receive there the first great tribute of public recognition which had been paid to him. He was entertained with great enthusiasm at a public banquet, voted the freedom of the city, and so overwhelmed with hospitalities that, notwithstanding his frank pleasure in these honours, he was glad to make his escape at last, and refreshed himself with a tour in the Highlands. These excitements may have intensified in him a desire which had for some time been active in his mind, and which in any case would have been kept alive by an incessant series of invitations. He had signed an

[1] As there is hardly a character in the whole world of fiction and the drama without some sort of a literary predecessor, so Dickens may have derived the first notion of Grip from the raven Ralpho—likewise the property of an idiot—who frightened Roderick Random and Strap out of their wits, and into the belief that he *was* the personage Grip so persistently declared himself to be.

agreement with his publishers for a new book before this desire took the shape of an actual resolution. There is no great difficulty in understanding why Dickens made up his mind to go to America, and thus to interrupt for the moment a course of life and work which was fast leading him on to great heights of fame and fortune. The question of international copyright alone would hardly have induced him to cross the seas. Probably he felt instinctively that to see men and cities was part of the training as well as of the recreation which his genius required. Dickens was by nature one of those artists who when at work always long to be in sympathy with their public, and to know it to be in sympathy with them. And hitherto he had not met more than part of his public of readers face to face.

CHAPTER III.

A JOURNEY across the Atlantic in midwinter is no child's-play even at the present day, when, bad though their passage may have been, few people would venture to confess doubts, as Dickens did, concerning the safety of such a voyage by steam in heavy weather. The travellers —for Dickens was accompanied by his wife—had an exceptionally rough crossing, the horrors of which he has described in his *American Notes.* His powers of observation were alive in the midst of the lethargy of sea-sickness, and when he could not watch others he found enough amusement in watching himself. At last, on January 28th, 1842, they found themselves in Boston harbour. Their stay in the United States lasted about four months, during which time they saw Boston, New York, Philadelphia, Baltimore, Washington, Richmond, Cincinnati, St. Louis, Chicago, and Buffalo. Then they passed by Niagara into Canada, and after a pleasant visit to Montreal, diversified by private theatricals with the officers there, were safe at home again in July.

Dickens had met with an enthusiastic welcome in every part of the States where he had not gone out of the way

E

of it; in New York, in particular, he had been fêted, with a fervour unique even in the history of American enthusiasms, under the resounding title of "the Guest of the Nation." Still, even this imposed no moral obligation upon him to take the advice tendered to him in America, and to avoid writing about that country—"we are so very suspicious." On the other hand, whatever might be his indignation at the obstinate unwillingness of the American public to be moved a hair's-breadth by his championship of the cause of international copyright,[1] this failure could not, in a mind so reasonable as his, have outweighed the remembrance of the kindness shown to him and to his fame. But the truth seems to be that he had, if not at first, at least very speedily, taken a dislike to American ways which proved too strong for him to the last. In strange lands, most of all in a country which, like the United States, is not in the least ashamed to be what it is, travellers are necessarily at the outset struck by details ; and Dickens' habit of minute observation was certain not to let him lose many of them. He was neither long enough in the country to study very closely, nor was it in his way to ponder very deeply, the problems involved in the existence of many of the institutions with which he found fault. Thus, he was indignant at the sight of slavery, and even ventured to "tell a piece of his mind" on the subject to a Judge in the South; but when, twenty years later, the great struggle came, at the root of which this question lay, his sympathies were with the cause of disunion and slavery in its conflict with the "mad and

[1] After dining at a party including the son of an eminent man of letters, he notes in his *Remembrancer* that he found the great man's son "decidedly lumpish," and appends the reflexion : "Copyrights need be hereditary, for genius isn't."

villainous " North. In short, his knowledge of America and its affairs was gained in such a way and under such circumstances as to entitle him, if he chose, to speak to the vast public which he commanded as an author, of men and manners as observed by him ; but he had no right to judge the destinies and denounce the character of a great people on evidence gathered in the course of a holiday tour.

Nor, indeed, did the *American Notes*, published by him after his return home, furnish any serious cause of offence. In an introductory chapter, which was judiciously suppressed, he had taken credit for the book as not having " a grain of any political ingredient in its whole composition." Indeed, the contents were rather disappointing from their meagreness. The author showed good taste in eschewing all reference to his personal reception, and good judgment in leaving the copyright question undiscussed. But though his descriptions were as vivid as usual—whether of the small steamboat, " of about half a pony power," on the Connecticut river, or of the dismal scenery on the Mississippi, " great father of rivers, who (praise be to Heaven) has no young children like him !"—and though some of the figure-sketches were touched off with the happiest of hands, yet the public, even in 1842, was desirous to learn something more about America than this. It is true that Dickens had, with his usual conscientiousness, examined and described various interesting public institutions in the States—prisons, asylums, and the like ; but the book was not a very full one ; it was hardly anything but a sketch-book, with more humour, but with infinitely less poetic spirit, than the *Sketch-book* of the illustrious American author, whose friendship had been one of the chief personal gains of Dickens' journey.

The *American Notes*, for which the letters to Forster
had furnished ample materials, were published in the year
of Dickens' return, after he had refreshed himself with a
merry Cornish trip in the company of his old friend, and
his two other intimates, " Stanny " and " Mac." But he
had not come home, as he had not gone out, to be idle.
On the first day of the following year, 1843, appeared the
first number of the story which was to furnish the real
casus discriminis between Dickens and the enemies, as
well no doubt as a very large proportion of the friends,
whom he had left behind him across the water. The
American scenes in *Martin Chuzzlewit* did not, it is true,
begin till the fifth number of the story; nor is it
probable from the accounts of the sale, which was much
smaller than Dickens had expected, that these particular episodes at first produced any strong feeling in the
English public. But the merits of the book gradually
obtained for it a popularity at home which has been
surpassed by that of but one or two other of Dickens'
works; and in proportion to this popularity was the
effect exercised by its American chapters. What that
effect has been, it would be hypocrisy to question.

Dickens, it is very clear, had been unable to resist the
temptation of at once drawing upon the vast addition to
his literary capital as a humourist. That the satire of
many of the American scenes in *Martin Chuzzlewit* is, as
satire, not less true than telling, it needs but a small
acquaintance with American journalism and oratory even at
the present day to perceive; and the heartrending history
of Eden, as a type of some of the settlements " vaunted
in England as a mine of Golden Hope," at least had the
warrant of something more than hearsay and a look in
passing. Nor, as has already been observed, would it have

been in accordance either with human nature, or with the fitness of things, had Dickens allowed his welcome in America to become to him (as he termed it in the suppressed Preface to the *Notes*) "an iron muzzle disguised beneath a flower or two." But the frankness, to say the least, of the mirror into which he now invited his late hosts to gaze, was not likely to produce grateful compliments to its presenter, nor was the effect softened by the despatch with which this *souvenir* of the "guest of the nation" was pressed upon its attention. No doubt it would have been easy to reflect that only the evil, not the good, sides of social life in America were held up to derision and contempt, and that an honourable American journalist had no more reason to resent the portraiture of Mr. Jefferson Brick than a virtuous English *paterfamilias* had to quarrel with that of Mr. Pecksniff. Unfortunately, offence is usually taken where offence is meant; and there can be little doubt as to the *animus* with which Dickens had written. Only two months after landing at Boston Dickens had declared to Macready, that "however much he liked the ingredients of this great dish, he could not but say that the dish itself went against the grain with him, and that he didn't like it." It was not, and could not be, pleasant for Americans to find the "*New York Sewer*, in its twelfth thousand, with a whole column of New Yorkers to be shown up, and all their names printed," introduced as the first expression of "the bubbling passions of their country;" or to be certified, apropos of a conversation among American "gentlemen" after dinner, that dollars, and dollars only, at the risk of honesty and honour, filled their souls. "No satirist," Martin Chuzzlewit is told by a candid and open-minded American, "could, I believe, breathe this air."

But satire in such passages as these, borders too closely on angry invective; and neither the irresistible force, nor the earnest pathos, of the details which follow, can clear away the suspicion that at the bottom lay a desire to depreciate. Nor was the general effect of the American episodes in *Martin Chuzzlewit* materially modified by their conclusion, to which, with the best of intentions, the author could not bring himself to give a genuinely complimentary turn. The Americans did not like all this, and could not be expected to like it. The tone of the whole satire was too savage, and its tenor was too hopelessly onesided, for it to pass unresented; while much in it was too near the truth to glance off harmless. It is well known that in time Dickens came himself to understand this. Before quitting America in 1868, he declared his intention to publish in every future edition of his *American Notes* and *Martin Chuzzlewit*, his testimony to the magnanimous cordiality of his second reception in the States, and to the amazing changes for the better which he had seen everywhere around him during his second sojourn in the country. But it is not likely that the postscript, all the more since it was added under circumstances so honourable to both sides, has undone, or will undo, the effect of the text. Very possibly the Americans may, in the eyes of the English people as well as in their own, cease to be chargeable with the faults and foibles satirised by Dickens; but the satire itself will live, and will continue to excite laughter and loathing, together with the other satire of the powerful book to which it belongs.

For in none of his books is that power, which at times filled their author himself with astonishment, more strikingly and abundantly revealed than in *The Life and*

Adventures of Martin Chuzzlewit. Never was his inventive
force more flexible and more at his command; yet
none of his books cost him more hard work. The very
names of hero and novel were only the final fortunate
choice out of a legion of notions; though "Pecksniff" as
well as "Charity" and "Mercy" ("not unholy names, I
hope," said Mr. Pecksniff to Mrs. Todgers) were first inspirations. The MS. text too is full of the outward signs of care.
But the author had his reward in the general impression
of finish which is conveyed by this book as compared
with its predecessors; so that *Martin Chuzzlewit* may
be described as already one of the masterpieces of
Dickens' maturity as a writer. Oddly enough, the one
part of the book which moves rather heavily is the opening chapter, an effort in the mock-heroic, probably suggested by the author's eighteenth century readings.

A more original work, however, than *Martin Chuzzlewit*
was never composed, or one which more freshly displays
the most characteristic qualities of its author's genius.
Though the actual construction of the story is anything
but faultless—for what could be more slender than the
thread by which the American interlude is attached to
the main action, or more wildly improbable than the
hazardous stratagem of old Martin upon which that
action turns?—yet it is so contrived as to fulfil the
author's avowed intention of exhibiting under various
forms the evil and the folly of selfishness. This vice is
capable of both serious and comic treatment, and commended itself in each aspect to Dickens as being essentially antagonistic to his moral and artistic ideals of
human life. A true comedy of humours thus unfolded
itself with the progress of his book, and one for which
the types had not been fetched from afar: "Your homes

the scene; yourselves the actors here" had been the motto
which he had at first intended to put upon his title-page.
Thus, while in "the old-established firm of Anthony
Chuzzlewit and Son" selfishness is cultivated as a growth
excellent in itself, and the son's sentiment, "Do other
men, for they would do you," is applauded by his
admiring father, in young Martin the vice rather resembles a weed strong and rank, yet not so strong but
that it gives way at last before a manly endeavour to
uproot it.   The character of the hero, though very far
from heroic, is worked out with that reliance upon the
fellow-feeling of candid readers which in our great
novelists of the eighteenth century has obtained sympathy
for much less engaging personages.   More especially is
the young man's loss of self-respect in the season of his
solitary wretchedness depicted with admirable feeling.
It would not, I think, be fanciful to assert that in this
story Dickens has with equal skill distinguished between
two species of unselfishness.   Mark Tapley's is the actively
unselfish nature, and though his reiteration of his guiding
motive is wearisome and occasionally absurd, yet the
power of coming out jolly under unpropitious circumstances is a genuinely English ideal of manly virtue.
Tom Pinch's character, on the other hand, is unselfish
from innate sweetness ; and never has the art of Dickens
drawn a type which, while closely approaching the border-
line of the grotesque, is yet so charmingly true to nature.

Grotesque characters proper are numerous enough in this
book, but all the others pale before the immortal presence
of Mrs. Gamp.   She has been traced to an original in real
life, but her literary right to stand on her own legs has
been most properly vindicated against any supposition of
likeness to the different type, the subject of Leigh Hunt's

Monthly Nurse,—a paper, by the way, distinguished by shrewdness as well as feeling. Imagination has never taken bolder flights than those requisite for the development of Mrs. Gamp's mental processes :

"And which of all them smoking monsters is the Ankworks boat, I wonder. Goodness me!" cried Mrs. Gamp.

"What boat did you want ?" asked Ruth.

"The Ankworks package," Mrs. Gamp replied. "I will not deceive you, my sweet. Why should I ?"

"That is the Antwerp packet in the middle," said Ruth.

"And I wish it was in Jonadge's belly, I do," cried Mrs. Gamp, appearing to confound the prophet with the whale in this miraculous aspiration.

A hardly inferior exertion of creative power was needed in order to fix in distinct forms the peculiarities of her diction, nay, to sustain the unique rhythm of her speech :

"I says to Mrs. Harris," Mrs. Gamp continued, " only t' other day, the last Monday fortnight as ever dawned upon this Piljian's Projiss of a mortal wale; I says to Mrs. Harris, when she says to me, 'Years and our trials, Mrs. Gamp, sets marks upon us all.' 'Say not the words, Mrs. Harris, if you and me is to be continual friends, for sech is not the case.'"

Yet the reality of Mrs. Gamp has been acknowledged to be such that she has been the death of her sisterhood in a great part (to say the least) of our hospital wards and sick rooms ; and as for her oddities of tongue, they are, with the exception of her boldest figures, but the glorified type of all the utterances heard to this day from charwomen, laundresses, and single gentlemen's housekeepers. Compared with her, even her friend and patron, Mr. Mould, and her admirer, Mr. Bailey, and in other parts of the book the low company at Todgers' and the fine company at Mr. Tigg Montague's sink into insignificance. The aged Chuffey is a grotesque study of a very different kind, of which the pathos never loses itself in exaggeration. As for Pecksniff, he is as far out of the range of grotesque, as, except when moralising over the banisters at Todgers', he is out of that of genial, characters. He is the richest comic type, while at the same time one of the truest, among the innumerable reproductions in English imaginative literature of our favourite national vice—hypocrisy. His friendliness is the very quintessence of falsehood: "Mr. Pinch," he cries to poor Tom over the currant wine and captain's biscuits, "if you spare the bottle, we shall quarrel!" His understanding with his daughters is the very perfection of guile, for they confide in him, even when ignorant of his intentions, because of their certainty "that in all he does, he has his purpose straight and full before him." And he is a man who understands the times as well as the land in which he lives; for, as M. Taine has admirably pointed out, where Tartuffe would have been full of religious phrases, Pecksniff presents himself as a humanitarian philosopher. Comic art has never more successfully fulfilled its highest task after its truest fashion than in this picture of the rise and fall of a creature, who never ceases to be laughable, and yet never ceases to be loathsome. Nothing is wanting in this wonderful book to attest the exuberance of its author's genius. The kindly poetic spirit of the Christmas books breathes in sweet Ruth Pinch; and the tragic power of the closing chapters of *Oliver Twist* is recalled by the picture of Jonas before and after his deed of blood. I say nothing of merely descriptive passages, though in none of his previous stories had Dickens so completely mastered the secret of describing scenery and weather in their relation to his action or his characters.

Martin Chuzzlewit ran its course of twenty monthly

numbers; but already a week or two before the appearance of the first of these, Dickens had bestowed upon the public, young and old, the earliest of his delightful *Christmas Books*. Among all his productions perhaps none connected him so closely, and as it were personally, with his readers. Nor could it well have been otherwise; since nowhere was he so directly intent upon promoting kindliness of feeling among men,—more especially goodwill, founded upon respect, towards the poor. Cheerfulness was, from his point of view, twin-sister to charity; and sulkiness, like selfishness, belonged, as an appropriate ort, to the dustheap of "Tom Tiddler's Ground." What more fit than that he should mingle such sentiments as these with the holly and the mistletoe of the only English holiday in which remains a vestige of religious and poetic feeling? Beyond all doubt there is much that is tedious in the *cultus* of Father Christmas, and there was yet more in the days when the lower classes in England had not yet come to look upon a sufficiency of periodical holidays as part of their democratic inheritance. But that Dickens should constitute himself its chief minister and interpreter was nothing but fit. Already one of the *Sketches* had commended a Christmas dinner at which a seat is not denied even to "poor Aunt Margaret;" and Mr. Pickwick had never been more himself than in the Christmas game of Blind-man's-buff at Dingley Dell, in which "the poor relations caught the people who they thought would like it," and, when the game flagged, "got caught themselves." But he now sought to reach the heart of the subject; and the freshness of his fancy enabled him delightfully to vary his illustrations of a text of which it can do no man harm to be reminded in as well as out of season.

Dickens' Christmas Books were published in the Christmas seasons of 1843–1846, and of 1848. If the palm is to be granted to any one among them above its fellows, few readers would hesitate, I think, to declare themselves in favour of *The Cricket on the Hearth*, as tender and delicate a domestic idyll as any literature can boast. But the informing spirit proper of these productions, the desire to stir up a feeling of benevolence, more especially towards the poor and lowly, nowhere shows itself more conspicuously than in the earliest, *A Christmas Carol in Prose*, and nowhere more combatively than in the second in date, the "Goblin Story" of *The Chimes*. Of the former its author declared that he "wept and laughed and wept again" over it, "and excited himself in a most extraordinary manner in the composition; and thinking thereof he walked about the black streets of London, fifteen and twenty miles many a night, when all the sober folks had gone to bed." Simple in its romantic design like one of Andersen's little tales, the *Christmas Carol* has never lost its hold upon a public in whom it has called forth Christmas thoughts which do not all centre on "holly, mistletoe, red berries, ivy, turkeys, geese, game, poultry, brawn, meat, pigs, sausages, oysters, pies, puddings, fruit, and punch;" and the Cratchit household, with Tiny Tim, who did NOT die, are living realities even to those who have not seen Mr. Toole—an actor after Dickens' own heart—as the father of the family, shivering in his half-yard of comforter.

In *The Chimes*, composed in self-absorbed solitude at Genoa, he imagined that "he had written a tremendous book, and knocked the *Carol* out of the field." Though the little work failed to make "the great uproar" he had confidently anticipated, its purpose was certainly

unmistakeable; but the effect of hard exaggerations such
as Mr. Filer and Alderman Cute, and of a burlesque
absurdity like Sir Joseph Bowley, was too dreary to be
counteracted by the more pleasing passages of the tale.
In his novel *Hard Times*, Dickens afterwards reproduced
some of the ideas, and repeated some of the artistic
mistakes, to be found in *The Chimes*, though the design
of the later work was necessarily of a more mixed kind.
The Christmas book has the tone of a *doctrinaire* protest
against *doctrinaires*, and, as Forster has pointed out, is
manifestly written under the influence of Carlyle. But
its main doctrine was one which Dickens lost no
opportunity of proclaiming, and which here breaks
forth in the form of an indignant appeal by Richard
Fern, the outlaw in spite of himself : " Gentlefolks, be not
hard upon the poor ! "   No feeling was more deeply
rooted in Dickens' heart than this ; nor could he forbear
expressing it by invective and satire as well as by
humorous and pathetic pictures of his clients, among
whom Trotty Veck too takes a representative place.

The Cricket on the Hearth, as a true work of art, is
not troubled about its moral, easily though half-a-dozen
plain morals might be drawn from it ; a purer and
more lightsome creation of the fancy has never been woven
out of homespun materials. Of the same imaginative
type, though not executed with a fineness so surpassing, is
The Battle of Life, the treatment of a fancy in which
Dickens appears to have taken great pleasure. Indeed,
he declared that he was " thoroughly wretched at having to
use the idea for so short a story." As it stands, it is a pretty
idyll of resignation, very poetical in tone as well as in
conception, though here and there, notwithstanding the
complaint just quoted, rather lengthy. It has been con-

jectured, with much probability, that the success which had attended dramatic versions of Dickens' previous Christmas Books caused "those admirable comedians, Mr. and Mrs. Keeley," to be in his mind "when he drew the charming characters of Britain and Clemency Newcome." At all events the pair serve as good old bits of English pottery to relieve the delicate Sèvres sentiment of Grace and Marion. In the last of Dickens' Christmas Books, *The Haunted Man and the Ghost's Bargain*, he returns once more to a machinery resembling those of the earliest. But the fancy on which the action turns is here more forced, and the truth which it illustrates is after all only a half-truth, unless taken as part of the greater truth, that the moral conditions of man's life are more easily marred than mended. Once more the strength of the book lies in its humorous side. The picture of the good Milly's humble proteges the Tetterby family is to remind us that happiness consists precisely in that which the poor and the rich may alike obtain, but which it is so difficult for the poor, amidst their shifts and shabbiness, to keep fresh and green. Even without the evil influence of an enchanted chemist, it is hard enough for the Mrs. Tetterbys of real life always to be ministering angels to their families; for the hand of every little Tetterby not occasionally to be against the other little Tetterbys, and even for a devoted Johnny's temper never to rise against Moloch. All the more is that to be cherished in the poor which makes them love one another.

More than one of these Christmas books, both the humour and the sentiment of which are so peculiarly English, was written on foreign soil. Dickens' general conceptions of life, not less than his literary individuality,

had been formed before he became a traveller and sojourner
in foreign lands. In Italy, as elsewhere, a man will, in a
sense, find only what he takes there. At all events the
changed life brought with it for Dickens, though not at
once, a refreshment and a brief repose which invigorated
him for some of the truest efforts of his genius. His
resolution to spend some time on the Continent had
not been taken rashly, although it was at least hastened
by business disappointments. He seems at this time
as was virtually inevitable, to have seen a good deal
of society in London, and more especially to have
become a welcome guest of Lady Blessington and
Count d'Orsay at Gore House. Moreover, his services
were beginning to be occasionally claimed as a
public speaker; and altogether he must have found
more of his time than he wished slipping through
his hands. Lastly, he very naturally desired to see
what was to be seen, and to enjoy what was to be
enjoyed, by one gifted with a sleepless observation and
animated by a genuine love of nature and art. The
letters, public and private, which he wrote from Italy,
are not among the most interesting productions of his
pen; even his humour seems now and then ill at ease
in them, and his descriptive power narrow in its range.
His eyes were occasionally veiled, as are those of most
travellers in quest of " first impressions." Thus I cannot
but think his picture of Naples inadequate, and that of
its population unjust. Again, although he may have told
the truth in asserting that the Eternal City, at first sight,
"looked like—I am half afraid to write the word—like
LONDON," and although his general description of Rome
has been pronounced correct by competent judgment, yet
it is impossible to ignore in it the undertone of Bow

excitement for his nightly walks in the London streets, he settled down to his task. I have already described the spirit in which he executed it. No sooner was the writing done, than the other half of his double artist-nature was seized with another craving. The rage which possesses authors to read their writings aloud to sympathising ears, if such can be found, is a well-worn theme of satire; but in Dickens, the actor was almost as strong as the author, and he could not withstand the desire to interpret in person what he had written, and to watch its effect with his own eyes and ears. In the first days of November, therefore, he set off from Genoa, and made his way home by Bologna, Venice, Milan, and the Simplon Pass. Of this journey, his *Pictures from Italy* contains the record, including a chapter about Venice, pitched in an unusually poetic key. But not all the memories of all the Doges could have stayed the execution of his set purpose. On the 30th of November he reached London, and on the 2nd of December he was reading the *Chimes*, from the proofs, to the group of friends immortalised in Maclise's inimitable sketch. Three days afterwards the reading was repeated to a slightly different audience; and, indeed, it would seem, from an enthusiastic postscript to a letter addressed to his wife, that he had read at least part of the book to Macready on the night before that of the first conclave. The distance was no doubt wide between the intimacy of these friendly readings and the stormy seas of public audiences; but, however unconsciously, the first step had been taken. It may be worth noticing, in connexion with this, that the scheme of a private dramatic performance, which was to occupy much of Dickens' "leisure" in the year following, was proposed for the first time on the occasion of the first reading of the *Chimes*. Before

Christmas he was back again in his "Italian bowers." If
the strain of his effort in writing the *Chimes* had been
severe, the holiday which followed was long.   In the later
winter and early spring of 1845 he and the ladies of his
family saw Rome and Naples, and in June their Italian
life came to an end, and they were in London before the
close of the month.   Projects of work remained in abeyance
until the absorbing fancy of a private play had been realised
with an earnestness such as only Dickens could carry into
his amusements, and into this particular amusement above
all others.   The play was *Every Man in his Humour*; the
theatre, the little house in Dean Street, of whose chequered
fortunes no theatrical history has succeeded in exhausting
the memories; and the manager was of course "Bobadil,"
as Dickens now took to signing himself.   His joking remark to Macready, that he "thought of changing his
present mode of life, and was open to an engagement,"
was after all not so very wide of the mark.   According to the inevitable rule in such things, he and his
friends—among whom Mark Lemon, Douglas Jerrold,
and Forster were conspicuous—were "induced" to repeat
their performance at a larger house for a public charity,
and later in the year they played *The Elder Brother* for
Miss Fanny Kelly's benefit.   Leigh Hunt, whose opinion
however could hardly fail to be influenced by the circumstances under which Ben Jonson's comedy was afterwards
performed by the amateurs, and who was no longer the
youthful Draco of the *News*, afterwards spoke very highly
of Dickens' Bobadil.   It had "a spirit in it of intellectual
apprehension beyond anything the existing stage has
shown."   His acting in the farce which followed, Leigh
Hunt thought "throughout admirable; quite rich and
filled up."

Christmas, 1845, had passed, and *The Cricket on the Hearth* had graced the festival, when an altogether new chapter in Dickens' life seemed about to open for him. The experience through which he now passed was one on which his biographer, for reasons easy to guess, has touched very slightly, while his *Letters* throw no additional light on it at all. Most people, I imagine, would decline to pronounce upon the qualifications requisite in an editor of a great political journal. Yet, literary power of a kind which acts upon the multitude rapidly and powerfully, habits of order so confirmed as to have almost become second nature, and an interest in the affairs of the nation fed by an ardent enthusiasm for its welfare—these would seem to go some way towards making up the list. Of all these qualifications Dickens at various times gave proof, and they sufficed in later years to make him the successful conductor of a weekly journal which aimed at the enlightenment hardly less than at the entertainment of no inconsiderable portion of the British public. But, in the first place, political journalism proper is a craft of which very few men have been known to become masters by intuition, and Dickens had as yet had no real experience of it. His zealous efforts as a reporter can hardly be taken into account here. He had for a short time edited a miscellany of amusement, and had failed to carry beyond a beginning the not very carefully considered scheme of another. Recently, he had resumed the old notion of *Master Humphrey's Clock* in a different shape; but nothing had come of his projected cheap weekly paper for the present, while its title, "*The Cricket,*" was reserved for a different use. Since his reporting days he had, however, now and then appeared among the lighter combatants of political litera-

expense ; and he was determined not to forfeit his inde-
pendence through accepting Government—by which I
hope he means Whig party—aid for meeting the cost of the
contest.   Still, in 1845, though slack of faith in the
"people who govern us," he had not yet become the
irreclaimable political sceptic of later days ; and without
being in any way bound to the Whigs, he had that
general confidence in Lord John Russell which was all
they could expect from their irregular followers.   As yet,
however, he had shown no sign of any special aptitude
or inclination for political work, though if he addressed
himself to questions affecting the health and happiness
of the humbler classes, he was certain to bring to them
the enthusiasm of a genuine sympathy.   And a question
of this kind was uppermost in Englishmen's minds in
this year 1845, when at last the time was drawing near
for the complete abolition of the tax upon the staple
article of the poor man's daily food.

The establishment of a new London morning paper, on
the scale to which those already in existence had attained,
was a serious matter in itself ; but it seems to have been
undertaken in no spirit of diffidence by the projectors and
first proprietors of the *Daily News*.   With the early
history of the experiment I cannot here concern myself ;
it is, however, an open secret that the rate of expenditure
of the new journal was at first on a most liberal, not to
say lavish, scale, and that the losses of the proprietors
were for many years very large indeed.   Established on
those principles of radicalism which, on the whole, it has
in both good and evil times consistently maintained, the
Daily News was to rise superior to the opportunism, if
not to the advertisements, of the *Times*, and to outstrip
the cautious steps of the Whig *Morning Chronicle*.

Special attention was to be given to those industrial
enterprises with which the world teemed in that speculative age, and no doubt also to those social questions
affecting the welfare and elevation of the masses and
the relations between employers and employed, which
were attracting more and more of the public attention.
But in the first instance the actual political situation
would oblige the new journal to direct the greater part
of its energies to one particular question, which had, in
truth, already been threshed out by the organs of public
opinion, and as to which the time for action had at last
arrived. No liberal journal projected in 1845, and started
early in 1846, could fail to concentrate its activity for a
time upon the question of the corn-laws, to which the
session of 1846 was to give the death-blow.

It is curious enough, on opening the first number of the
Daily News, dated January 21st, 1846, to find oneself
transplanted into the midst of one of the most memorable
episodes of our more recent political history. The very
advertisements of subscriptions to the Anti-Corn-Law
League, with the good old Manchester names figuring
conspicuously among them, have a historic interest;
and the report of a disputation on free trade at Norwich,
in which all the hits are made by Mr. Cobden, another
report of a great London meeting on the same subject,
and some verses concerning the people's want of its bread,
probably written by Mr. Charles Mackay, occupy an entire
page of the paper. Railway news and accounts of railway meetings fill about the same space; while the foreign
news is extremely meagre. There remain the leading
articles, four in number—of which three are on the
burning question of the day—and the first of a series of
Travelling Letters written on the Road, by Charles Dickens

(the Avignon chapter in the *Pictures from Italy*).[1] The
hand of the editor is traceable only in this *feuilleton* and
in the opening article of the new paper.   On internal
evidence I conclude that this article, which has little
to distinguish it from similar manifestoes, unless it be a
moderation of tone that would not have suited Captain
Shandon, was not written by Dickens alone or unassisted.
But his hand is traceable in the concluding paragraphs,
which contain the following wordy but spirited assertion
of a cause that Dickens lost no opportunity of advocating :

We seek, so far as in us lies, to elevate the character of the
Public Press in England.   We believe it would attain a much
higher position, and that those who wield its powers would be
infinitely more respected as a class, and an important one, if it
were purged of a disposition to sordid attacks *upon itself*, which
only prevails in England and America.   We discern nothing in
the editorial plural that justifies a gentleman, or body of gentlemen, in discarding a gentleman's forbearance and responsibility, and venting ungenerous spleen against a rival, by a
perversion of a great power—a power, however, which is only
great so long as it is good and honest.   The stamp on newspapers
is not like the stamp on universal medicine-bottles, which licenses
anything, however false and monstrous; and we are sure this
misuse of it, in any notorious case, not only offends and repels
right-minded men in that particular instance, but naturally,
though unjustly, involves the whole Press, as a pursuit or profession, in the feeling so awakened, and places the character of
all who are associated with it at a great disadvantage.

---

[1] By an odd coincidence, not less than four out of the six
theatres advertising their performances in this first number of the
Daily News announce each a different adaptation of *The Cricket
on the Hearth*.   Among the curiosities of the casts are observable :
at the Adelphi, Wright as Tilly Slowboy, and at the Haymarket
Buckstone in the same character, with William Farren as Caleb
Plummer.   The latter part is taken at the Princess's by Compton,
Mrs. Stirling playing Dot.   At the Lyceum, Mr., Mrs., and Miss
Mary Keeley, and Mr. Emery appear in the piece.

Entering on this adventure of a new daily journal in a spirit of honourable competition and hope of public usefulness, we seek, in our new station, at once to preserve our own self-respect, and to be respected, for ourselves and for it, by our readers. Therefore, we beg them to receive, in this our first number, the assurance that no recognition or interchange of trade abuse, by us, shall be the destruction of either sentiment ; and that we intend proceeding on our way, and theirs, without stooping to any such flowers by the roadside.

I am unable to say how many days it was after the appearance of this first number that Dickens, or the proprietors of the journal, or, as seems most likely, both sides simultaneously, began to consider the expediency of ending the connexion between them. He was " revolving plans for quitting the paper" on January 30th, and resigned his editorship on February 9th following. In the interval, with the exception of two or three more of the *Travelling Letters*, very few signs of his hand appear in the journal. The number of January 24th, however, contains an editorial contribution, in the shape of "a new song, but an old story," concerning *The British Lion*, his accomplishment of eating Corn-Law Leagues, his principal keeper, *Wan Humbug*, and so forth. This it would be cruel to unearth. A more important indication of a line of writing that his example may have helped to domesticate in the *Daily News* appears in the number of February 4th, which contains a long letter, with his signature, urging the claims of Ragged Schools, and giving a graphic account of his visit to one in Saffron Hill. After he had placed his resignation in the hands of the proprietors, and was merely holding on at his post till the time of his actual withdrawal, he was naturally not anxious to increase the number of his contributions. The *Hymn of the Wiltshire Labourers*—which appeared on

February 14th—is, of course, an echo of the popular cry
of the day ; but the subtler pathos of Dickens never found
its way into his verse.   The most important, and so far as
I know the last, of his contributions to the *Daily News*,
consisted of a series of three letters (March 9th, 13th, and
16th) on capital punishment. It was a question which much
occupied him at various times of his life, and on which it
cannot be shown that he really changed his opinions. The
letters in the *Daily News*, based in part on the arguments
of one of the ablest men of his day, the "unlucky"
Mr. Wakefield, are an interesting contribution to the
subject ; and the first of them, with its Hogarthian sketch
of the temptation and fall of Thomas Hocker, Sunday-
school teacher and murderer, would be worth reprinting
as an example of Dickens' masterly use of the argument
ex concreto.

The few traditions which linger in the *Daily News*
office concerning Dickens as editor of the paper, agree
with the conjecture that his labours on its behalf were
limited, or very nearly so, to the few pieces enumerated
above.   Of course there must have been some inevitable
business ; but of this much may have been taken off his
hands by his sub-editor, Mr. W. H. Wills, who afterwards became his *alter ego* at the office of his own weekly
journal and his intimate personal friend.   In the days of
the first infancy of the *Daily News*, Mr. Britton, the
present publisher of that journal, was attached to the
editor as his personal office attendant ; and he re-
members very vividly what little there can have been
to remember about Dickens' performance of his functions.   His habit, following a famous precedent, was
to make up for coming late—usually about half-past
ten P.M.—by going away early—usually not long after

midnight.   There were frequently sounds of merriment,
if not of modest revelry, audible from the little room
at the office in Lombard Street, where the editor sat
in conclave with Douglas Jerrold and one or two other
intimates.   Mr. Britton is not sure that the work did
not sometimes begin *after the editor had left*; but at all
events he cannot recollect that Dickens ever wrote anything
at the office—that he ever for instance wrote about a
debate that had taken place in Parliament on the same
night.   And he sums up his reminiscences by declaring his
conviction that Dickens was "not a newspaper man, at
least not when in 'the chair.'"   And so Dickens seems
on this occasion to have concluded; for when, not long
after quitting the paper, he republished with additions the
Travelling Letters which during his conduct of it had
been its principal ornaments, he spoke of "a brief mistake
he had made, not long ago, in disturbing the old relations
between himself and his readers, and departing for a
moment from his old pursuits."   He had been virtually
out of "the chair" almost as soon as he had taken it;
his successor, but only for a few months, was his friend
Forster.

Never has captive released made a more eager or a
better use of his recovered freedom.   Before the summer
had fairly set in, Dickens had let his house, and was
travelling with his family up the Rhine towards Switzerland.   This was, I think, Dickens' only passage through
Germany, which in language and literature remained a
terra incognita to him, while in various ways so well
known to his friendly rivals, Lord Lytton and Thackeray.
He was on the track of poor Thomas Hood's old
journeyings, whose facetious recollections of Rhineland
he had some years before reviewed in a spirit of admira-

tion rather for the author than for the book, funny as it is.
His point of destination was Lausanne, where he had
resolved to establish his household for the summer, and
where by the middle of June they were most agreeably
settled in a little villa or cottage which did not belie
its name of Rosemont, and from which they looked upon
the lake and the mighty Alpine chain beyond.   If Rome
had reminded Dickens of London, the green woods near
Lausanne recalled to him his Kentish glades; but he had
the fullest sense and the truest enjoyment of the grandeurs
of Alpine scenery, and lost no opportunity of becoming
acquainted with them.   Thus his letters contain an admirable description (not untinged with satire) of a trip to the
Great St. Bernard and its convent, many years afterwards
reproduced in one of the few enjoyable chapters of the
Second Part of *Little Dorrit*.   More interesting, however,
because more characteristic, is the freshness and candour
with which in Switzerland, where by most English visitors
the native inhabitants are "taken for granted," he set
himself to observe, and, so far as he could, to appreciate,
the people among whom he was a temporary resident. His
solutions of some of the political difficulties, which were
mostly connected with religious differences, at that time
rife in Switzerland, are palpably one-sided. But the gene-
rosity of spirit which reveals itself in his kindly recognition of the fine qualities of the people around him,
is akin to what was best and noblest in Dickens.

He had, at the same time, been peculiarly fortunate in
finding at Lausanne a circle of pleasant acquaintances,
to whom he dedicated the Christmas book which he wrote
among the roses and the foliage of his lake-side cottage.
Of course *The Battle of Life* was read aloud by its
author to so kindly an audience.   The day of parting,

him more than its *salons,* more even than its theatres.
They are so to a larger number of Englishmen than that
which cares to confess it, but Dickens would have been the
last to disown the impeachment. They were the proper
sphere for his powers of humorous observation, as he afterwards showed in more than one descriptive paper as true
to life as any of his London *Sketches.* And, moreover,
he *needed* the streets for the work which he had in hand.
Dombey and Son had been begun at Rosemont, and the
first of its twenty monthly numbers had been published
in October, 1846. No reader of the book is likely to
forget how, after writing the chapter which relates the
death of little Paul, Dickens during the greater part of
the night wandered restlessly with a heavy heart about
the Paris streets. Sooner, however, than he had intended,
his residence abroad had to come to a close; and early in
1847 he and his family were again in London.

Dombey and Son has, perhaps, been more criticised
than any other among the stories of its author; and yet
it certainly is not the one which has been least admired,
or least loved. Dickens himself, in the brief preface
which he afterwards prefixed to the story, assumed a half-
defiant air which sits ill upon the most successful author,
but which occasionally he was tempted to assume. Before
condescending to defend the character of Mr. Dombey
as in accordance with both probability and experience,
he "made so bold as to believe that the faculty (or the
habit) of correctly observing the characters of men is a rare
one." Yet, though the drawing of this character is only
one of the points which have been objected against the
story, not only did the book at the time of publication
far surpass its predecessor in popularity, but it has, I
believe, always preserved to itself a special congregation

of enthusiastic admirers. Manifestly, this novel is one
of its author's most ambitious endeavours. In it, more
distinctly even than in *Chuzzlewit*, he has chosen for his
theme one of the chief vices of human nature, and has
striven to show what pride cannot achieve, what it cannot
conquer, what it cannot withstand. This central idea
gives to the story, throughout a most varied succession
of scenes, a unity of action to be found in few of Dickens'
earlier works. On the other hand, *Dombey and Son*
shares with these earlier productions, and with its successor, *David Copperfield*, the freshness of invention and
spontaneous flow of both humour and pathos which at
times are wanting in the more powerfully conceived and
more carefully constructed romances of Dickens' later
years. If there be any force at all in the common remark,
that the most interesting part of the book ends together
with the life of little Paul, the censure falls upon the
whole design of the author. Little Paul, in something
besides the ordinary meaning of the words, was born
to die ; and though, like the writer, most readers may
have dreaded the hour which was to put an end to that
frail life, yet in this case there could be no question—
such as was possible in the story of Little Nell—of any
other issue. Indeed, deep as is the pathos of the closing
scene, its beauty is even surpassed by those which precede it. In death itself there is release for a child as
for a man, and for those sitting by the pillow of the
patient; but it is the gradual approach of death which
seems hardest of all for the watchers to bear; it is the
sinking of hope which seems even sadder than its
extinction. What old fashion could that be, Paul
wondered with a palpitating heart, that was so visibly
expressed in him, so plainly seen by so many people ?

Every heart is softened and every eye dimmed, as the innocent child passes on his way to his grave. The hand of God's angel is on him; he is no longer altogether of this world. The imagination which could picture and present this mysterious haze of feeling, through which the narrative moves, half like a reality, half like a dream, is that of a true poet, and of a great one.

What even the loss of his son could not effect in Mr. Dombey is to be accomplished in the progress of the story by a yet stronger agency than sorrow. His pride is to be humbled to the dust, where he is to be sought and raised up by the love of his despised and ill-used daughter. Upon the relations between this pair, accordingly, it was necessary for the author to expend the greatest care, and upon the treatment of those relations the criticism to which the character of Mr. Dombey has been so largely subjected must substantially turn. The unfavourable judgments passed upon it have, in my opinion, not been altogether unjust. The problem obviously was to show how the father's cold indifference towards the daughter gradually becomes jealousy, as he finds that upon her is concentrated, first, the love of his innocent little son, and then that of his haughty second wife; and how hereupon this jealousy deepens into hate. But, unless we are to suppose that Mr. Dombey hated his daughter from the first, the disfavour shown by him on her account to young Walter Gay remains without adequate explanation. His dislike of Florence is not manifestly founded upon his jealousy of what Mrs. Chick calls her brother's " infatuation " for her; and the main motives at work in the unhappy man are either not very skilfully kept asunder, or not very intelligibly intermixed. Nor are the later stages of the relations between father and daughter

altogether satisfactorily conceived.   The momentary yield-
ing of Mr. Dombey, after his "coming home" with his
new wife, is natural and touching; but his threat to visit
his daughter with the consequences of her stepmother's
conduct is sheer brutality.   The passage in which
Mr. Dombey's ultimatum to Mrs. Dombey is conveyed
by him in her presence through a third person, is so
artificial as to fall not very far short of absurdity.   The
closing scene which leads to the flight of Florence is undeniably powerful; but it is the developement of the
relations between the pair, in which the art of the author
is in my judgment occasionally at fault.

As to the general effect of the latter part of the story
—or rather of its main plot—which again has been
condemned as melodramatic and unnatural, a distinction
should be drawn between its incidents and its characters.
Neither Edith Dombey nor Mr. Carker is a character of real
life.   The pride of the former comes very near to bad breed-
ing, and her lapses into sentiment seem artificial lapses.
How differently Thackeray would have managed the "high
words" between her and her frivolous mother; how differently, for that matter, he *has* managed a not altogether dis-
similar scene in the *Newcomes* between Ethel Newcome and
old Lady Kew! As for Mr. Carker, with his white teeth and
glistening gums, who calls his unhappy brother "Spaniel,"
and contemplates a life of sensual ease in Sicily, he has
the semi-reality of the stage.   Possibly, the French stage
had helped to suggest the *scène de la pièce* between the
fugitives at Dijon—an effective situation, but one which
many a novelist might have worked out not less skilfully
than Dickens.   His own master-hand, however, reasserts
itself in the wondrously powerful narrative of Carker's
flight and death.   Here again, he excites terror—as in

the same book he had evoked pity—by foreshadowing, without prematurely revealing, the end. We know what the morning is to bring which rises in awful tranquillity over the victim of his own sins; and, as in Turner's wild but powerful picture, the engine made by the hand of man for peaceful purposes seems a living agent of wrath.[1]

No other of Dickens' books is more abundantly stocked than this with genuinely comic characters; but nearly all of them, in accordance with the pathetic tone which is struck at the outset, and which never dies out till the story has run its course, are in a more subdued strain of humour. Lord Jeffrey was, I think, warranted in his astonishment that Dickens should devote so much pains to characters like Mrs. Chick and Miss Tox; probably the habit remained with him from his earliest times of authorship, when he had not always distinguished very accurately between the humorous and the *bizarre*. But Polly and the Toodles household, Mrs. Pipchin and her "select infantine boarding-house," and the whole of Doctor Blimber's establishment, from the Doctor himself down to Mr. Toots, and up again, in the scale of intellect, to Mr. Feeder, B.A., are among the most admirable of all the great humorist's creations. Against this ample provision for her poor little brother's nursing and training Florence has to set but her one Susan Nipper; but she is a host in herself, an absolutely original character among the thousands of *soubrettes* that are known to comedy and fiction, and one of the best

[1] It is perhaps worth pointing out, though it is not surprising, that Dickens had a strong sense of what I may call the poetry of the railway train. Of the effect of the weird *Signalman's Story* in one of his Christmas numbers, it is not very easy to rid oneself. There are excellent descriptions of the *rapidity* of a railway journey in the first chapter of *The Lazy Tour*, and in another *Household Words* paper, called *A Flight*.

G

tonic mixtures ever composed out of much humour and not
a few grains of pathos.   Her tartness has a cooling flavour
of its own ; but it is the Mrs. Pipchinses only upon whom
she acts, as their type acted upon her, "like early goose-
berries."   Of course she has a favourite figure of speech
belonging to herself, which rhetoricians would probably
class among the figures " working by surplusage : "

"Your Toxes and your Chickses may draw out my two front
double teeth, Mrs. Richards, but that's no reason why I need
offer 'em the whole set."

Dickens was to fall very largely into this habit of
"labelling" his characters, as it has been called, by particular
tricks or terms of speech ; and there is a certain excess in
this direction already in *Dombey and Son*, where not
only Miss Nipper and Captain Cuttle and Mr. Toots, but
Major Bagstock too and Cousin Feenix, are thus furnished
forth.   But the invention is still so fresh and the play of
humour so varied, that this mannerism cannot be said as
yet seriously to disturb them.   A romantic charm of a
peculiar kind clings to honest Captain Cuttle and the quaint
home over which he mounts guard during the absence of its
owner.   The nautical colouring and concomitant fun apart—
for only Smollett could have drawn Jack Bunsby's fellow,
though the character in his hands would have been differently accentuated—Dickens has never approached
more nearly to the manner of Sir Walter Scott than
in this singularly attractive part of his book.   Elsewhere
the story passes into that sphere of society in describing
which Dickens was, as a novelist, rarely very successful.
But though Edith is cold and unreal, there is, it cannot
be denied, human nature in the pigments and figments
of her hideous old mother; and, to outward appearance at

all events, the counterparts of her apoplectic admirer, Major Bagstock, still pace those pavements and promenades which it suits them to frequent. Cousin Feenix is likewise very far from impossible, and is besides extremely delightful—and a good fellow too at bottom, so that the sting of the satire is here taken away. On the other hand, the meeting between the *sacs et parchemins* at Mr. Dombey's house is quite out of focus.

The book has other heights and depths, and pleasant and unpleasant parts and passages. But enough has been said to recall the exuberant creative force, and the marvellous strength of pathos and humour which *Dombey and Son* proves that Dickens, now near the very height of his powers as a writer of fiction, possessed. In one of his public readings many years afterwards, when he was reciting the adventures of Little Dombey, he narrates that "a very good fellow," whom he noticed in the stalls, could not refrain from wiping the tears out of his eyes as often as he thought that Toots was coming on. And just as Toots had become a reality to this good fellow, so Toots and Toots' little friend, and divers other personages in this story, have become realities to half the world that reads the English tongue, and to many besides. What higher praise could be given to this wonderful book? Of all the works of its author none has more powerfully and more permanently taken hold of the imagination of its readers. Though he conjured up only pictures familiar to us from the aspect of our own streets and our own homes, he too wielded a wizard's wand.

After the success of *Dombey*, it might have seemed that nothing further was wanting to crown the prosperity of Dickens' literary career. While the publication of this

to fight a match for the champion's belt, and he calls it 'Play.'
Play!'" exclaimed Thomas Idle, scornfully contemplating his one
boot in the air; "you can't play. You don't know what it is.
You make work of everything!"

"A man," added the same easy philosopher, " who can
do nothing by halves appears to me to be a fearful man."
And as at all times in Dickens' life, so most emphatically in
these years when his physical powers seemed ready to
meet every demand, and the elasticity of his mind seemed
equal to every effort, he did nothing by halves. Within
this short space of time, not only did he write his best
book, and conduct a weekly journal of solid merit through
its most trying stage, but he also established his reputation as one of the best "unpolitical" speakers in the
country ; and as an amateur actor and manager successfully weathered what may be called three theatrical
seasons, to the labours and glories of which it would
be difficult to find a parallel even in the records of that
most exacting of all social amusements. One likes to
think of him in these years of vigorous manhood, no
longer the fair youth with the flowing locks of Maclise's
charming portrait, but not yet, I suppose, altogether the
commanding and rather stern presence of later years.
Mr. Frith's portrait was not painted till 1859, by which
time the face occasionally had a more set expression, and
the entire personality a more weather-beaten appearance
than this well-known picture suggests. But even eight
years before this date, when Dickens was acting in
Lord Lytton's comedy the part of a young man of mode,
Mr. Sala's well-known comparison of his outward man to
"some prosperous sea-captain home from a sea-voyage,"
was thought applicable to him by another shrewd observer,
Mr. R. H. Horne, who says that, fashionable "make-up"

notwithstanding, "he presented a figure that would have made a good portrait of a Dutch privateer after having taken a capital prize." And in 1856, Ary Scheffer, to whom when sitting for his portrait he had excused himself for being a difficult subject, "received the apology as strictly his due, and said with a vexed air: 'At this moment, *mon cher* Dickens, you look more like an energetic Dutch admiral than anything else;' for which I apologised again." In 1853, in the sympathetic neighbourhood of Boulogne, he was "growing a moustache," and, by 1856, a beard of the *Henri Quatre* type had been added; but even before that time we may well believe that he was, as Mr. Sala says, "one of the few men whose individuality was not effaced by the mournful conventionality of evening dress." Even in morning dress he unconsciously contrived, born actor as he was, to have something unusual about him; and, if report speaks the truth, even at the seaside, when most prodigal of ease, he was careful to dress the character.

The five years of which more especially I am speaking, brought him repeatedly face to face with the public, and within hearing of the applause that was becoming more and more of a necessity to him. They were thus unmistakeably among the very happiest years of his life. The shadow that was to fall upon his home can hardly yet have been visible even in the dim distance. For this the young voices were too many and too fresh around him behind the garden-wall in Devonshire Terrace, and among the autumnal corn on the cliffs at Broadstairs. "They are all in great force," he writes to his wife, in September, 1850, and "much excited with the expectation of receiving you on Friday;" and I only wish I had space to quote the special report sent on this occasion to

the absent mother concerning her precocious three-year-old.
What sorrowful experiences he in these years underwent,
were such as few men escape among the chances of life.
In 1848 he lost the sister who had been the companion of
his earliest days, and three years later his father, whom
he had learnt to respect as well as love. Not long
afterwards his little Dora, the youngest of his flock, was
suddenly taken from him. Meanwhile, his old friends
clung to him. Indeed, I never heard that he lost the
affection of anyone who had been attached to him; and
though the circle of his real intimates was never greatly
widened, yet he was on friendly or even familiar terms
with many whose names belong to the history of their
times. Among these were the late Lord Lytton—then
Sir Edward Bulwer Lytton—whose splendid abilities were
still devoted mainly to literary labours, and between whom
and Dickens there were more points of contrast than might
at first sight appear. Of Thackeray, too, he seems to have
been coming to know more; and with Leech, more especially
during a summer sojourn of both their families at Bonchurch,
in 1849, he grew intimate. Mr. Monckton Milnes—then
and since as Lord Houghton, *semper amicus, semper hospes*
both to successful merit and to honest endeavour—Lord
Carlisle, and others who adorned the great world under
more than one of its aspects, were of course welcome friends
and acquaintances; and even Carlyle occasionally found his
way to the house of his stanch admirer, though he might
declare that he was, in the language of Mr. Peggotty's
housekeeper, " a lorn lone creature, and everything went
contrairy with him."

It is not very easy to describe the personal habits of a
man who is found seeing the spring in at Brighton
and the autumn out at Broadstairs, and in the interval

" strolling " through the chief towns of the kingdom at
the head of a large company of ladies and gentlemen,
according to the description which he put into Mrs.
Gamp's mouth, " with a great box of papers under his
arm, a-talking to everybody wery indistinct, and exciting of himself dreadful." But since under ordinary
circumstances he made, even in outward matters and
arrangements of detail, a home for himself wherever he
was, and as a rule cared little for the society of companions
whose ideas and ways of life were foreign to his own,
certain habits had become second nature to him, and to
others he adhered with sophistical tenacity. He was an
early riser, if for no other reason, because every man in
whose work imagination plays its part must sometimes
be alone; and Dickens has told us that there was to
him something incomparably solemn in the still solitude
of the morning. But it was only exceptionally, and when
hard pressed by the necessities of his literary labours,
that he wrote before breakfast; in general he was contented with the ordinary working hours of the morning,
not often writing after luncheon, and, except in early life,
never in the evening. Ordinarily, when engaged on a
work of fiction, he considered three of his not very large
MS. pages a good, and four an excellent, day's work;
and, while very careful in making his corrections clear
and unmistakeable, he never rewrote what a morning's
labour had ultimately produced. On the other hand,
he was frequently slow in beginning a story, being, as
he himself says, affected by something like despondency
at such times, or, as he elsewhere humorously puts it,
" going round and round the idea, as you see a bird in his
cage go about and about his sugar before he touches it."
A temperate liver, he was at the same time a zealous

devotee of bodily exercise. He had not as yet given up
riding, and is found, in 1848, spending the whole of a
March day, with Forster, Leech, and Mark Lemon, in
riding over every part of Salisbury Plain. But walking
exercise was at once his forte and his fanaticism ; he is
said to have constructed for himself a theory that, to every
portion of the day given to intellectual labour should cor-
respond an equal number of hours spent in walking ; and
frequently no doubt he gave up his morning's chapter
before he had begun it, " entirely persuading himself that
he was under a moral obligation" to do his twenty miles
on the road. By day he found in the London thorough-
fares stimulative variety, and at a later date he states it
to be " one of his fancies that even his idlest walk must
have its appointed destination ;" and by night, in seasons
of intellectual excitement, he found in these same streets
the refreshment of isolation among crowds. But the
walks he loved best were long stretches on the cliffs or
across the downs by the sea, where, following the track
of his " breathers," one half expects to meet him coming
along against the wind at four-and-a-half miles an hour,
the very embodiment of energy and brimful of life.

And besides this energy he carried with him, where-
soever he pitched his tent, what was the second cause
of his extraordinary success in so much of the business of
life as it fell to him to perform. He hated disorder as
Sir Artegall hated injustice ; and if there was anything
against which he took up his parable with burning indignation, it was slovenliness, and half-done work, and
"shoddiness" of all kinds. His love of order made him
always the most regular of men. " Everything with him,"
Miss Hogarth told me, " went as by clockwork ; his movements, his absences from home, and the times of his return

were all fixed beforehand, and it was seldom that he failed
to adhere to what he had fixed." Like most men endowed
with a superfluity of energy, he prided himself on his
punctuality; he could not live in a room or in a house
till he had put every piece of furniture into its proper
place, nor could he begin to work till all his writing-gear
was at hand, with no item missing or misplaced. Yet he
did not, like so many, combine with these habits and
tendencies a saving disposition; "no man," he said of
himself, "attaches less importance to the possession of
money, or less disparagement to the want of it, than I do."
His circumstances, though easy, were never such as to
warrant a display to which perhaps certain qualities of his
character might have inclined him; even at a much later
date he described himself—rather oddly perhaps—as "a
man of moderate savings, always supporting a very ex-
pensive public position." But, so far as I can gather, he
never had a reasonable want which he could not and did
not satisfy, though at the same time he cared for very
few of the pursuits or amusements that are apt to drain
much larger resources than his. He never had to think
twice about country or seaside quarters; wherever it
might suit his purpose or fancy to choose them, at one
of his south-coast haunts or, for his wife's health, at
Malvern, thither he went; and when the whim seized him
for a trip *en garçon* to any part of England or to Paris, he
had only to bid the infallible Anne pack his trunk. He
was a provident as well as an affectionate father; but the
cost of educating his numerous family seems to have
caused him no serious anxiety; in 1849 he sent his eldest
son to Eton. And while he had sworn a kind of *vendetta*
against begging-letter writers, and afterwards used to
parry the attacks of his pertinacious enemies by means

of carefully-prepared written forms, his hand seems to
have been at all times open for charity.

Some of these personal characteristics of Dickens were
to be brought out with remarkable vividness during the
period of his life which forms the special subject of the
present chapter.   Never was he more thoroughly himself
than as a theatrical manager and actor, surrounded by
congenial associates.   He starred it to his heart's content
at the country seat of his kind Lausanne friends, Mr. and
Mrs. Watson.   But the first occasion on which he became
publicly known in both the above-mentioned capacities,
was the reproduction of the amateur performance of *Every
Man in his Humour*.   This time the audiences were to
be in Manchester and Liverpool, where it was hoped that
a golden harvest might be reaped for Leigh Hunt, who
was at that time in sore straits.   As it chanced, a civil-
list pension was just about this time—1847—conferred
upon the most unaffectedly graceful of all modern
writers of English verse.   It was accordingly resolved to
divert part of the proceeds of the undertaking in favour
of a worthy playwright, the author of *Paul Pry*.   The
comedy was acted with brilliant success at Manchester,
on July 26th, and at Liverpool two days later; and then
the "managerial miseries," which Dickens had enjoyed
with his whole heart and soul, were over for the nonce.
Already, however, in the following year, 1848, an excellent reason was found for their recommencement; and
nine performances of Ben Jonson's play, this time alter-
nated with *The Merry Wives of Windsor*, were given by
Dickens' "company of amateurs"—the expression is his
own—at the Haymarket, and in the theatres of five of the
largest towns in the kingdom, for the benefit of Sheridan
Knowles.   Nothing could have been more honourable

than Dickens' readiness to serve the interests of an actor
with whom, but for his own generous temper, he would
only a few months before have been involved in a
wordy quarrel.   In *The Merry Wives*, the manager
acted Justice Shallow to Mark Lemon's Falstaff.
Dame Quickly was played by Mrs. Cowden Clarke,
who speedily became a favourite correspondent of
Dickens.   But the climax of these excitements arrived
in the year of wonders, 1851, when, with a flourish
of trumpets resounding through the world of fashion
as well as of letters, the comedy, *Not so Bad as We
Seem*, written for the occasion by Bulwer Lytton, was
performed under Dickens' management at Devonshire
House, in the presence of the Queen, for the benefit of
the Guild of Literature and Art.   The object was a noble
one, though the ultimate result of the scheme has been an
almost pitiable failure; and nothing was spared, by the
host or the actors, to make the effect worthy of it.   While
some of the most popular men of letters took parts in the
clever and effective play, its scenery was painted by some of
the most eminent among English artists.   Dickens was fired
by the ardour of the enterprise, and proceeding on his principle that the performance could not possibly "be a success
if the smallest peppercorn of arrangement were omitted,"
covered himself and his associates with glory.   From
Devonshire House play and theatre were transferred
to the Hanover Square Rooms, where the farce of
Mr. Nightingale's Diary was included in the performance, of which some vivid reminiscences have been
published by one of the few survivors of that noble
company, Mr. R. H. Horne.   Other accounts corrobo-
rate his recollections of the farce, which was the
triumph of "gag," and would have been reckoned a

voluntary labour on Dickens' part.   Not that he was one of
those to whom the task of occasionally addressing a public
audience is a pain or even a burden.   Indeed, he was a
born orator; for he possessed both that strong and elastic
imaginative power which enables a man to place himself
at once in sympathy with his audience, and that gift of
speech, pointed, playful, and where necessary impetuous,
which pleads well in any assembly for any cause.   He
had moreover the personal qualifications of a handsome
manly presence, a sympathetic eye, and a fine flexible
voice which, as his own hints on public speaking show,
he managed with care and intelligence.   He had, he says,
" fought with beasts (oratorically) in divers arenas."   But
though a speaker in whom ease bred force, and force ease,
he was the reverse of a mere builder of phrases and
weaver of periods.   " Mere holding forth," he declared,
" I utterly detest, abominate, and abjure."   His innate
hatred of talk for mere talk's sake had doubtless been
intensified by his early reporting experiences, and by what
had become his stereotyped notion of our parliamentary
system.   At the Administration Reform meeting in 1855
he stated that he had never before attended a public
meeting.   On the other hand, he had been for already
several years in great request for meetings of a
different kind, concerned with the establishment or
advancement of educational or charitable institutions
in London and other great towns of the country.
His addresses from the chair were often of remarkable excellence ; and this not merely because crowded
halls and increased subscription-lists were their con-
comitants, and because the happiness of his humour—
never out of season, and even on such occasions often
singularly prompt—sent everyone home in good spirits.

and pathos on behalf of his clients, the poor actors, when, unknown to him, a little child of his own was lying dead at home. But in these years of his life, as indeed at all times, his voice was at the service of such causes as had his sympathy; it was heard at Birmingham, at Leeds, at Glasgow; distance was of little moment to his energetic nature; and as to trouble, how could he do anything by halves?

There was yet a third kind of activity, distinct from that of literary work pure and simple, in which Dickens in these years for the first time systematically engaged. It has been seen how he had long cherished the notion of a periodical conducted by himself, and marked by a unity of design which should make it in a more than ordinary sense his own paper. With a genius like his, which attached itself to the concrete, very much depended at the outset upon the choice of a title. *The Cricket* could not serve again, and for some time the notion of an omnipresent *Shadow*, with something, if possible, tacked to it "expressing the notion of its being cheerful, useful, and always welcome,"seemed to promise excellently. For a rather less ambitious design, however, a rather less ambitious title was sought, and at last fortunately found, in the phrase, rendered proverbial by Shakespeare, *"Household Words."* "We hope," he wrote a few weeks before the first number appeared, on March 30th, 1850, "to do some solid good, and we mean to be as cheery and pleasant as we can." But *Household Words*, which in form and in cost was to be a paper for the multitude, was to be something more than agreeable and useful and cheap. It was to help in casting out the many devils that had taken up their abode in popular periodical literature, the "bastards of the Mountain," and the foul fiends who

H

dealt in infamous scurrility, and to do this with the aid
of a charm more potent than the most lucid argument and
the most abundant facts. " In the bosoms of the young
and old, of the well-to-do and of the poor," says the
Preliminary Word in the first number, "we would
tenderly cherish that light of fancy which is inherent
in the human breast." To this purpose it was the
editor's constant and deliberate endeavour to bind his
paper. "KEEP 'HOUSEHOLD WORDS' IMAGINATIVE !" is
the "solemn and continual Conductorial Injunction"
which three years after the foundation of the journal he
impresses, with the artful aid of capitals, upon his faithful
coadjutor, Mr. W. H. Wills. In his own contributions
he was not forgetful of this maxim, and the most important of them, the serial story, *Hard Times*, was written
with the express intention of pointing it as a moral.

There are, I suppose, in addition to the many mysterious
functions performed by the editor of a literary journal,
two of the very highest significance ; in the first place,
the choice of his contributors, and then, if the expression
may be used, the management of them. In both respects
but one opinion seems to exist of Dickens' admirable
qualities as an editor. Out of the many contributors
to *Household Words*, and its kindred successor, *All the
Year Round*—some of whom are happily still among
living writers—it would be invidious to select for mention
a few in proof of the editor's discrimination. But it
will not be forgotten that the first number of the
earlier journal contained the beginning of a tale by
Mrs. Gaskell, whose name will long remain a household word in England, both North and South. And a
periodical could hardly be deemed one-sided which included among its contributors scholars and writers of

the distinction belonging to the names of Forster and Mr. Henry Morley, together with humorous observers of men and things such as Mr. Sala and Albert Smith. On the other hand, *Household Words* had what every literary journal ought to have, an individuality of its own; and this individuality was of course that of its editor. The mannerisms of Dickens' style afterwards came to be imitated by some among his contributors; but the general unity perceptible in the journal was the natural and legitimate result of the fact that it stood under the independent control of a vigorous editor, assisted by a sub-editor—Mr. W. H. Wills—of rare trustworthiness. Dickens had a keen eye for selecting subjects from a definite field, a ready skill for shaping, if necessary, the articles accepted by him, and a genius for providing them with expressive and attractive titles. Fiction and poetry apart, these articles have mostly a social character or bearing, although they often deviate into the pleasant paths of literature or art; and usually, but by no means always, the scenes or associations with which they connect themselves are of England, English.

Nothing could surpass the unflagging courtesy shown by Dickens towards his contributors, great or small, old or new, and his patient interest in their endeavours, while he conducted *Household Words*, and afterwards *All the Year Round*. Of this there is evidence enough to make the records of the office in Wellington Street a pleasant page in the history of journalism. He valued a good workman when he found him, and was far too reasonable and generous to put his own stamp upon all the good metal that passed through his hands. Even in his Christmas Numbers he left the utmost possible freedom

to his associates.   Where he altered or modified it was as
one who had come to know the pulse of the public ; and he
was not less considerate with novices, than he was frank and
explicit with experts, in the writer's art.   The articles in his
journal being anonymous, he was not tempted to use names
as baits for the public, though many who wrote for him
were men or women of high literary reputation.   And he
kept his doors open.   While some editors deem it their
duty to ward off would-be contributors, as some ministers
of state think it theirs to get rid of deputations, Dickens
sought to ignore instead of jealously guarding the boundaries
of professional literature.   Nothing in this way ever gave
him greater delight than to have welcomed and published
several poems sent to him under a feigned name, but which
he afterwards discovered to be the first-fruits of the
charming poetical talent of Miss Adelaide Procter, the
daughter of his old friend " Barry Cornwall."

In the preparation of his own papers, or of those
which, like the Christmas Numbers, he composed con-
jointly with one or more of his familiars, he spared no
labour and thought no toil too great.   At times, of course,
he, like all periodical writers who cannot be merry every
Wednesday or caustic every Saturday, felt the pressure
of the screw—" as to two comic articles," he exclaims on
one occasion, " or two any sort of articles, out of me,
that's the intensest extreme of no-goism."   But, as a rule,
no great writer ever ran more gaily under his self-imposed
yoke.   His " Uncommercial Travels," as he at a later
date happily christened them, familiarised him with
whatever parts or aspects of London his long walks had
still left unexplored ; and he was as conscientious in
hunting up the details of a complicated subject as in
finding out the secrets of an obscure pursuit or trade.

Accomplished antiquarians and "commissioners" assisted
him in his labours; but he was no *roi fainéant* on
the editorial sofa which he so complacently describes.
Whether he was taking *A Walk in a Workhouse*, or
knocking at the door of another with the supernumerary
waifs in Whitechapel, or *On* (night) *Duty with Inspector
Field* among the worst of the London slums, he was
always ready to see with his own eyes ; after which the
photographic power of his pen seemed always capable
of doing the rest. Occasionally he treats topics more
properly journalistic, but he is most delightful when he
takes his ease in his *English* or his *French Watering
Place*, or carries his readers with him on *A Flight to
Paris*, bringing before them, as it were, in breathless
succession, every inch of the familiar journey. Happiest
of all is he when, with his friend Mr. Wilkie Collins—
this, however, not until the autumn of 1857—he starts
on *The Lazy Tour of Two Idle Apprentices*, the earlier
chapters of which furnish some of the best specimens of
his most humorous prose. Neither at the same time does
he forget himself to enforce the claim of his journal
to strengthen the imaginary side of literature. In an
assumed character he allows a veteran poet to carry him
By Rail to Parnassus, and even good-humouredly banters
an old friend, George Cruikshank, for having committed
Frauds on the Fairies by re-editing legendary lore with
the view of inculcating the principle of Total Abstinence.

Such, then, were some of the channels in which the
intense mental and physical energy of Dickens found a
congenial outlet in these busy years. Yet in the very
midst of this multifarious activity the mysterious and
controlling power of his genius enabled him to collect
himself for the composition of a work of fiction which, as

aware of the pang it must have cost Dickens to lay bare, though to unsuspecting eyes, the story of experiences which he had hitherto kept all but absolutely secret, and to which his own mind could not recur without a quivering sensitiveness. No reader could trace, as the memory of Dickens always must have traced, some of the most vivid of those experiences, imbued though they were with the tints of a delightfully playful humour, in the doings and dealings of Mr. Wilkins Micawber, whose original, by a strange coincidence, was passing tranquilly away out of life, while his comic counterpart was blossoming into a whimsical immortality. And no reader could divine, what very probably even the author may hardly have ventured to confess to himself, that in the lovely little idyll of the loves of Doady and Dora—with Jip, as Dora's father might have said, intervening—there were, besides the reminiscences of an innocent juvenile amour, the vestiges of a man's unconfessed though not altogether unrepressed disappointment—the sense that "there was always something wanting." But in order to be affected by a personal or autobiographical element in a fiction or poem, it is by no means necessary to be aware of its actual bearing and character, or even of its very existence; *Amelia* would gain little by illustrative notes concerning the experiences of the first Mrs. Fielding. To excite in a work of fiction the peculiar kind of interest of which I am speaking, the existence of an autobiographical substratum need not be apparent in it, nor need its presence be even suspected. Enough, if it be *there.* But it had far better be away altogether, unless the novelist has so thoroughly fused this particular stream of metal with the mass filling his mould that the result is an integral artistic whole. Such was, however, the case with *David Copperfield,* which of all Dickens' fictions is on the whole the most perfect as a work of art. Personal reminiscences which lay deep in the author's breast are, as effects, harmonised with local associations old and new. Thus Yarmouth, painted in the story with singular poetic truthfulness, had only quite recently been seen by Dickens for the first time, on a holiday trip. His imagination still subdued to itself all the elements with which he worked; and, whatever may be thought of the construction of this story, none of his other books equals it in that harmony of tone which no artist can secure unless by recasting all his materials.

As to the construction of *David Copperfield*, however, I frankly confess that I perceive no serious fault in it. It is a story with a plot, and not merely a string of adventures and experiences, like little Davy's old favourites upstairs at Blunderstone. In the conduct of this plot blemishes may here and there occur. The boy's flight from London, and the direction which it takes, are insufficiently accounted for. A certain amount of obscurity as well perhaps as of improbability, pervades the relations between Uriah and the victim, round whom the unspeakable slimy thing writhes and wriggles. On the other hand, the mere conduct of the story has much that is beautiful in it. Thus there is real art in the way in which the scene of Barkis' death—written with admirable moderation—prepares for the " greater loss " at hand for the mourning family. And in the entire treatment of his hero's double love story, Dickens has, to my mind, avoided that discord which—in spite of himself, jars upon the reader both in *Esmond* and in *Adam Bede*. The best constructed part of *David Copperfield* is, however, unmistakeably the story of Little Emily and her kins-folk. This is most skilfully interwoven with the personal

experiences of David, of which—except in its very begin-
nings—it forms no integral part; and throughout the reader
is haunted by a presentiment of the coming catastrophe,
though unable to divine the tragic force and justice of its
actual accomplishment. A touch altered here and there
in Steerforth, with the Rosa Dartle episode excluded or
greatly reduced, and this part of *David Copperfield* might
challenge comparison as to workmanship with the whole
literature of modern fiction.

Of the idyll of Davy and Dora—what shall I say? Its
earliest stages are full of the gayest comedy. What, for
instance, could surpass the history of the picnic—where
was it? perhaps it was near Guildford. At that feast an
imaginary rival, " Red Whisker," made the salad—how
could they eat it?—and " voted himself into the charge
of the wine-cellar, which he constructed, *being an ingenious
beast*, in the hollow trunk of a tree." Better still are the
backward ripples in the course of true love; best of all
the deep wisdom of Miss Mills, in whose nature mental
trial and suffering supplied, in some measure, the place
of years. In the narrative of the young housekeeping,
David's real trouble is most skilfully mingled with the
comic woes of the situation; and thus the idyll almost
imperceptibly passes into the last phase, where the clouds
dissolve in a rain of tears. The genius which conceived
and executed these closing scenes was touched by a pity
towards the fictitious creatures of his own imagination,
which melted his own heart; and thus his pathos is here
irresistible.

The inventive power of Dickens in none of his other
books indulged itself so abundantly in the creation of
eccentric characters, but neither was it in any so admirably
tempered by taste and feeling. It contains no character

which could strictly be called grotesque, unless it be little Miss Mowcher. Most of her outward peculiarities Dickens had copied from a living original, but receiving a remonstrance from the latter he good-humouredly altered the use he had intended to make of the character, and thereby spoilt what there was in it—not much in my opinion—to spoil. Mr. Dick belongs to a species of eccentric personages—mad people in a word—for which Dickens as a writer had a curious liking; but though there is consequently no true humour in this character, it helps to bring out the latent tenderness in another. David's Aunt is a figure which none but a true humorist such as Sterne or Dickens could have drawn, and she must have sprung from the author's brain armed *cap-à-pie* as she appeared in her garden before his little double. Yet even Miss Betsey Trotwood was not altogether a creation of the fancy, for at Broadstairs the locality is still pointed out where the "one great outrage of her life" was daily renewed. In the other chief characters of this story the author seems to rely entirely on natural truthfulness. He must have had many opportunities of noting the ways of seamen and fishermen, but the occupants of the old boat near Yarmouth possess the typical characteristics with which the experience and the imagination of centuries have agreed to credit the "salt" division of mankind. Again, he had had his own experience of shabby-genteel life, and of the struggle which he had himself seen a happy and a buoyant temperament maintaining against a sea of trouble. But Mr. Micawber, whatever features may have been transferred to him, is the type of a whole race of men who will not vanish from the face of the earth so long as the hope which lives eternal in the human breast is only temporarily suspended by the laws of debtor and creditor, and is always capable of revival with the aid of a bowl of milk-punch. A kindlier and a merrier, a more humorous and a more genuine character was never conceived than this; and if anything was wanted to complete the comicality of the conception, it was the wife of his bosom with the twins at her own, and her mind made up *not* to desert Mr. Micawber. Delightful too in his way, though of a class more common in Dickens, is Tommy Traddles, the genial picture of whose married life in chambers in Gray's Inn, with the dearest girl in the world and her five sisters, including the beauty, on a visit, may have been suggested by kindly personal reminiscences of youthful days. In contrast to these characters, the shambling, fawning, villainous hypocrisy of Uriah Heep is a piece of intense and elaborate workmanship, almost cruelly done without being overdone. It was in his figures of hypocrites that Dickens' satirical power most diversely displayed itself; and by the side of Uriah Heep in this story, literally so in the prison-scene at the close, stands another species of the race, the valet Littimer, a sketch which Thackeray himself could not have surpassed.

Thus, then, I must leave the book, with its wealth of pathos and humour, with the glow of youth still tinging its pages, but with the gentler mood of manhood pervading it from first to last. The *reality* of *David Copperfield* is, perhaps, the first feature in it likely to strike the reader new to its charms; but a closer acquaintance will produce, and familiarity will enhance, the sense of its wonderful *art*. Nothing will ever destroy the popularity of a work of which it can truly be said that, while offering to his muse a gift not less beautiful than precious, its author put into it his life's blood.

CHAPTER V.

CHANGES.

1852--1858.

I HAVE spoken of both the intellectual and the physical vigour of Charles Dickens as at their height in the years of which the most enduring fruit was the most delightful of all his fictions. But there was no break in his activity after the achievement of this or any other of his literary successes, and he was never harder at work than during the seven years of which I am about to speak, although in this period also occasionally he was to be found hard at play. Its beginning saw him settled in his new and cheerfully-furnished abode at Tavistock House, of which he had taken possession in October, 1851. At its close he was master of the country residence which had been the dream of his childhood, but he had become a stranger to that tranquillity of mind without which no man's house is truly his home. Gradually, but surely, things had then, or a little before, come to such a pass that he wrote to his faithful friend: "I am become incapable of rest. I am quite confident I should rust, break and die, if I spared myself. Much better to die, doing. What I am in that way, nature made me first, and my way of life has of late, alas! confirmed." Early in 1852, the youngest of his children had been born to him—the boy whose babyhood once more revived in him a tenderness the depth of which no eccentric humours and fantastic *sobriquets* could conceal. In May, 1858, he had separated from the mother of his children, and though self-sacrificing affection was at hand to watch over them and him, yet that domestic life of which he had become the prophet and poet to hundreds of thousands was in its fairest and fullest form at an end for himself.

In the earlier of these years, Dickens' movements were still very much of the same kind, and varied much after the same fashion as in the period described in my last chapter. In 1852 the series of amateur performances in the country was completed; but time was found for a summer residence in Camden Crescent, Dover. During his stay there, and during most of his working hours in this and the following year—the spring of which was partly spent at Brighton—he was engaged upon his new story, *Bleak House,* published in numbers dating from March, 1852, to September, 1853. "To let you into a secret," he had written to his lively friend, Miss Mary Boyle, from Dover, "I am not quite sure that I ever did like, or ever shall like anything quite so well as *Copperfield.* But I foresee, I think, some very good things in *Bleak House.*" There is no reason to believe that, by the general public, this novel was at the time of its publication a whit less favourably judged or less eagerly read than its predecessor. According to the author's own testimony, it "took extraordinarily, especially during the last five or six months" of its issue, and "retained its immense circulation from the first, beating dear old *Copperfield* by a round ten thousand or more." To this day the book has its stanch friends, some of whom would perhaps be slow to confess by which of the elements in the story they are most forcibly attracted. On the other hitherto more or less consciously adopted—the novel of adventure, of which the person of the hero, rather than the machinery of the plot, forms the connecting element. It may be that the influence of Mr. Wilkie Collins was already strong upon him, and that the younger writer, whom Dickens was about this time praising for his unlikeness to the "conceited idiots who suppose that volumes are to be tossed off like pancakes," was already teaching something to, as well as learning something from, the elder. It may also be that the criticism which as editor of *Household Words* Dickens was now in the habit of judiciously applying to the fictions of others, unconsciously affected his own methods and processes. Certain it is that from this point of view *Bleak House* may be said to begin a new series among his works of fiction. The great Chancery suit and the fortunes of those concerned in it are not a disconnected background from which the mystery of Lady Dedlock's secret stands forth in relief; but the two main parts of the story are skilfully interwoven as in a Spanish double-plot. Nor is the success of the general action materially affected by the circumstance that the tone of Esther Summerson's diary is not altogether true. At the same time, there is indisputably some unevenness in the construction of *Bleak House*. It drags, and drags very perceptibly, in some of its earlier parts. On the other hand, the interest of the reader is strongly revived, when that popular favourite, Mr. Inspector Bucket, appears on the scene, and when, more especially in the admirably vivid narrative of Esther's journey with the detective, the nearness of the catastrophe exercises its exciting influence. Some of the machinery, moreover—such as the Smallweed family's part in the plot—is tiresome; and particular incidents are intolerably horrible or absurd—

such as, on the one hand, the spontaneous combustion (which is proved possible by the analogy of historical facts !), and on the other, the intrusion of the oil-grinding Mr. Chadband into the solemn presence of Sir Leicester Dedlock's grief. But in general the parts of the narrative are well knit together; and there is a subtle skill in the way in which the two main parts of the story converge towards their common close.

The idea of making an impersonal object like a great Chancery suit the centre round which a large and manifold group of characters revolves, seems to savour of a drama rather than of a story. No doubt the theme suggested itself to Dickens with a very real purpose, and on the basis of facts which he might well think warranted him in his treatment of it; for, true artist though he was, the thought of exposing some national defect, of helping to bring about some real reform, was always paramount in his mind over any mere literary conception. *Primâ facie*, at least, and with all due deference to Chancery judges and eminent silk gowns like Mr. Blowers, the length of Chancery suits was a real public grievance, as well as a frequent private calamity. But even as a mere artistic notion, the idea of Jarndyce *v.* Jarndyce as diversely affecting those who lived by it, those who rebelled against it, those who died of it, was in its way of unique force; and while Dickens never brought to any other of his subjects so useful a knowledge of its external details—in times gone by he had served a " Kenge and Carboys " of his own—hardly any one of those subjects suggested so wide a variety of aspects for characteristic treatment.

For never before had his versatility in drawing character filled his canvas with so multitudinous and so various a host of personages. The legal profession, with its servitors and hangers-on of every degree, occupies the centre of the picture. In this group no figure is more deserving of admiration than that of Mr. Tulkinghorn, the eminently respectable family solicitor at whose very funeral, by a four-wheeled affliction, the goodwill of the aristocracy manifests itself. We learn very little about him, and probably care less ; but he interests us precisely as we should be interested by the real old family lawyer, about whom we might know and care equally little, were we to find him alone in the twilight, drinking his ancient port in his frescoed chamber in those fields where the shepherds play on Chancery pipes that have no stop. (Mr. Forster, by the way, omitted to point out to his readers, what the piety of American research has since put on record, that Mr. Tulkinghorn's house was a picture of the biographer's own residence.) The portrait of Mr. Vholes, who supports an unassailable but unenviable professional reputation for the sake of " the three dear girls at home," and a father whom he has to support "in the Vale of Taunton," is less attractive ; but nothing could be more in its place in the story than the clammy tenacity of this legal ghoul and his " dead glove." Lower down in the great system of the law, we come upon Mr. Guppy and his fellows, the very quintessence of cockney vulgarity, seasoned with a flavour of legal sharpness without which the rankness of the mixture would be incomplete. To the legal group Miss Flite, whose original, if I remember right, used to haunt the Temple as well as the precincts of the Chancery courts, may likewise be said to belong. She is quite legitimately introduced into the story—which cannot be said of all Dickens' madmen —because her madness associates itself with its main theme.

I

Much admiration has been bestowed upon the figures of an eccentric by- or under-plot in this story, in which the family of the Jellybys and the august Mr. Turvey-drop are, actively, or by passive endurance, engaged. The philanthropic section of *le monde où l'on s'ennuie* has never been satirised more tellingly, and, it must be added, more bitterly. Perhaps at the time of the publication of *Bleak House* the activity of our Mrs. Jellybys took a wider and more cosmopolitan sweep than in later days; for we read at the end of Esther's diary how Mrs. Jellyby "has been disappointed in Borrioboola Gha, which turned out a failure in consequence of the King of Borrioboola wanting to sell everybody—who survived the climate—for Rum; but she has taken up with the rights of women to sit in Parliament, and Caddy tells me it is a mission involving more correspondence than the old one." But Mrs. Jellyby's interference in the affairs of other people is after all hurtful only because in busying herself with theirs she forgets her own. The truly offensive bene-factress of her fellow-creatures is Mrs. Pardiggle, who, maxim in mouth and tract in hand, turns everything she approaches to stone. Among her victims are her own children, including Alfred, aged five, who has been in-duced to take an oath "never to use tobacco in any form."

The particular vein of feeling that led Dickens to the delineation of these satirical figures was one which never ran dry with him, and which suggested some forcible-feeble satire in his very last fiction. I call it a vein of feeling only; for he could hardly have argued in cold blood that the efforts which he ridicules were not mis-represented as a whole by his satire. When poor Jo on his deathbed is "asked whether he ever knew a prayer," and replies that he could never make anything out of those spoken by the gentlemen who " came down Tom-all-Alone's a-prayin'," but who " mostly sed as the t'other wuns prayed wrong," the author brings a charge which he might not have found it easy to substantiate. Yet —with the exception of such isolated passages—the figure of Jo is in truth one of the most powerful protests that have been put forward on behalf of the friendless outcasts of our streets. Nor did the romantic element in the conception interfere with the effect of the realistic. If Jo, who seems at first to have been intended to be one of the main figures of the story, is in Dickens' best pathetic manner, the Bagnet family is in his happiest vein of quiet humour. Mr. Inspector Bucket, though not altogether free from mannerism, well deserves the popularity which he obtained. For this character, as the pages of *Household Words* testify, Dickens had made many studies in real life. The detective police-officer had at that time not yet become a standing figure of fiction and the drama, nor had the detective of real life begun to destroy the illusion.

Bleak House was least of all among the novels hitherto published by its author obnoxious to the charge persistently brought against him, that he was doomed to failure in his attempts to draw characters taken from any but the lower spheres of life—in his attempts, in short, to draw ladies and gentlemen. To begin with, one of the most interesting characters in the book—indeed, in its relation to the main idea of the story, the most interesting of all—is the youthful hero, if he is to be so called, Richard Carson. From the very nature of the conception, the character is passive only; but the art and feeling are in their way unsurpassed with which the gradual collapse of a fine

nature is here exhibited. Sir Leicester Dedlock, in some
measure intended as a type of his class, has been condemned as wooden and unnatural; and no doubt the
machinery of that part of the story in which he is concerned creaks before it gets under way. On the other
hand, after the catastrophe has overwhelmed him and
his house, he becomes a really fine picture, unmarred by
any Grandisonianisms in either thought or phrase, of a
true gentleman, bowed but not warped by distress. Sir
Leicester's relatives, both dead and living; Volumnia's
sprightly ancestress on the wall, and that "fair Dedlock"
herself; the whole cousinhood, debilitated and otherwise,
but of one mind on such points as William Buffy's blame-
worthy neglect of his duty *when in office*; all these make
up a very probable picture of a house great enough—or
thinking itself great enough—to look at the affairs of the
world from the family point of view. In Lady Dedlock
alone a failure must be admitted; but she, with her
wicked double, the uncanny French maid Hortense,
exists only for the sake of the plot.

With all its merits, *Bleak House* has little of that charm
which belongs to so many of Dickens' earlier stories, and
to *David Copperfield* above all. In part at least, this
may be due to the excessive severity of the task which
Dickens had set himself in *Bleak House*; for hardly any
other of his works is constructed on so large a scale, or
contains so many characters organically connected with
the progress of its plot; and in part, again, to the half-
didactic half-satirical purport of the story, which weighs
heavily on the writer. An overstrained tone announces itself
on the very first page; an opening full of power—indeed,
of genius; but pitched in a key which we feel at once
will not, without effort, be maintained. On the second

page the prose has actually become verse ; or how else
can one describe part of the following apostrophe ?

" This is the Court of Chancery, which has its decaying houses
and its blighted lands in every shire ; which has its worn-out
lunatic in every madhouse, and its dead in every churchyard ;
which has its ruined suitor with his slipshod heels and thread-
bare dress, borrowing and begging through the round of every
man's acquaintance ; which gives to monied might the means
abundantly of wearing out the right ; which so exhausts finances,
patience, courage, hope ; so overthrows the brain and breaks the
heart, that there is not an honourable man among its practi-
tioners who would not give—who does not often give—the
warning, ' Suffer any wrong that can be done you, rather than
come here ! ' "

It was possibly with some thought of giving to
Bleak House also, though in a different way, the close
relation to his experiences of living men to which
David Copperfield had owed so much, that Dickens
introduced into it two *portraits*. Doubtless, at first, his
intention had by no means gone so far as this. His
constant counsellor always disliked his mixing up in his
fictitious characters any personal reminiscences of particular
men, experience having shown that in such cases the whole
character came out *more like* than the author was aware.
Nor can Dickens himself have failed to understand how
such an experiment is always tempting, and always
dangerous, how it is often irreconcileable with good
feeling, and quite as often with good taste. In *Bleak
House*, however, it occurred to him to introduce likenesses
of two living men, both more or less well known to the
public and to himself ; and both of individualities too
clearly marked for a portrait, or even a caricature, of
either to be easily mistaken. Of that art of mystification
which the authors of both English and French *romans à*

clef have since practised with so much transient success, he was no master, and fortunately so : for what could be more ridiculous than that the reader's interest in a character should be stimulated, first, by its being evidently the late Lord P–lm–rst–n, or the P—— of O——, and then by its being no less evidently somebody else? It should be added that neither of the two portrait characters in *Bleak House* possesses the least importance for the conduct of the story, so that there is nothing to justify their introduction except whatever excellence may belong to them in themselves.

Lawrence Boythorn is described by Mr. Sydney Colvin as drawn from Walter Savage Landor with his intellectual greatness left out. It was of course unlikely that his intellectual greatness should be left in, the intention obviously being to reproduce what was eccentric in the ways and manner, with a suggestion of what was noble in the character, of Dickens' famous friend. Whether, had he attempted to do so, Dickens could have drawn a picture of the whole Landor, is another question. Landor, who could put into a classic dialogue that sense of the *naïf* to which Dickens is generally a stranger, yet passionately admired the most *sentimental* of all his young friend's poetic figures ; and it might almost be said that the intellectual natures of the two men were drawn together by the force of contrast. They appear to have first become intimate with one another during Landor's residence at Bath—which began in 1837—and they frequently met at Gore House. At a celebration of the poet's birthday in his lodgings at Bath, so Forster tells us in his biography of Landor, "the fancy which took the form of Little Nell in the *Curiosity Shop* first dawned on the genius of its creator." In Landor's spacious mind there

features in the portrait. Nor does it contradict the
substantial truthfulness of Dickens' own statement,
published in *All the Year Round* after Leigh Hunt's
death, on the appearance of the new edition of the
Autobiography with Thornton Hunt's admirable introduction. While, Dickens then wrote, " he yielded to the
temptation of too often making the character speak like
his old friend," yet " he no more thought, God forgive
him ! that the admired original would ever be charged
with the imaginary vices of the fictitious creature, than
he had himself ever thought of charging the blood of
Desdemona and Othello on the innocent Academy model
who sat for Iago's leg in the picture. Even as to the mere
occasional manner," he declared that he had "altered the
whole of that part of the text, when two intimate friends
of Leigh Hunt—both still living—discovered too strong a
resemblance to his ' way.' " But, while accepting this
statement, and suppressing a regret that after discovering
the dangerous closeness of the resemblance Dickens should
have, quite at the end of the story, introduced a satirical
reference to Harold Skimpole's autobiography—Leigh
Hunt's having been published only a year or two before—
one must confess that the explanation only helps to prove
the rashness of the offence. While intending the portrait
to keep its own secret from the general public, Dickens
at the same time must have wished to gratify a few keen-
sighted friends. In March, 1852, he writes to Forster,
evidently in reference to the apprehensions of his correspondent : " Browne has done Skimpole, and helped to
make him singularly unlike the great original." The
" great original " was a man for whom, both before and
after this untoward incident in the relations between them,
Dickens professed a warm regard, and who, to judge from

the testimony of those who knew him well,[1] and from his
unaffected narrative of his own life, abundantly deserved
it.   A perusal of Leigh Hunt's *Autobiography* suffices to
show that he used to talk in Skimpole's manner, and even
to write in it; that he was at one period of his life altogether ignorant of money matters, and that he cultivated
cheerfulness on principle.   But it likewise shows that
his ignorance of business was acknowledged by him as a
misfortune in which he was very far from exulting.   "Do
I boast of this ignorance?" he writes.   "Alas! I have no
such respect for the pedantry of absurdity as that.   I
blush for it, and I only record it out of a sheer painful
movement of conscience, as a warning to those young
authors who might be led to look upon such folly as a fine
thing, which at all events is what I never thought it
myself."   On the other hand, as his son showed, his
cheerfulness, which was not inconsistent with a natural
proneness to intervals of melancholy, rested on grounds
which were the result of a fine as well as healthy morality.
"The value of cheerful opinions," he wrote, in words em-
bodying a moral than Dickens himself was never weary of
enforcing, "is inestimable; they will retain a sort of
heaven round a man, when everything else might fail him,
and consequently they ought to be religiously inculcated
upon his children."   At the same time, no quality was more
conspicuous in his life than his readiness for hard work,
even under the most depressing circumstances; and no
feature was more marked in his moral character than his

---

[1] Among these is Mr. Alexander Ireland, the author of the
Bibliography of Leigh Hunt and Hazlitt, who has kindly communicated to me part of his collections concerning the former.
The tittle-tattle against Leigh Hunt repeated by Lord Macaulay
is, on the face of it, unworthy of notice.

conscientiousness. " In the midst of the sorest tempta-
tions," Dickens wrote of him, " he maintained his honesty
unblemished by a single stain ; and in all public and private
transactions he was the very soul of truth and honour."
To mix up with the outward traits of such a man the
detestable obliquities of Harold Skimpole was an experiment paradoxical even as a mere piece of character-drawing.
The merely literary result is a failure, while a wound was
needlessly inflicted, if not upon Leigh Hunt himself, at
least upon all who cherished his friendship or good name.
Dickens seems honestly and deeply to have regretted what
he had done, and the extremely tasteful little tribute to
Leigh Hunt's poetic gifts, which, some years before the
death of the latter, Dickens wrote for *Household Words*,[1]
must have partaken of the nature of an *amende honorable*.
Neither his subsequent repudiation of unfriendly intentions, nor his earlier exertions on Leigh Hunt's behalf, are
to be overlooked, but they cannot undo a mistake which
forms an unfortunate incident in Dickens' literary life,
singularly free though that life as a whole is from the
miseries of personal quarrels, and all the pettinesses with
which the world of letters is too familiar.

While Dickens was engaged upon a literary work such
as would have absorbed the intellectual energies of most
men, he not only wrote occasionally for his journal, but
also dictated for publication in it the successive portions
of a book altogether outside his usual range of authorship.
This was *A Child's History of England*, the only one of
his works that was not written by his own hand. A
history of England, written by Charles Dickens for his
own or anyone else's children, was sure to be a different
work from one written under similar circumstances by

[1] *By Rail to Parnassus*, June 16, 1855.

Mr. Freeman or the late M. Guizot. The book, though it cannot be called a success, is however by no means devoid of interest. Just ten years earlier he had written, and printed, a history of England for the benefit of his eldest son, then a hopeful student of the age of five, which was composed, as he informed Douglas Jerrold at the time, "in the exact spirit" of that advanced politician's paper, "for I don't know what I should do if he were to get hold of any Conservative or High Church notions; and the best way of guarding against any such horrible result is, I take it, to wring the parrots' necks in his very cradle." The *Child's History of England* is written in the same spirit, and illustrates more directly, and, it must be added, more coarsely than any of Dickens' other works, his hatred of ecclesiasticism of all kinds. Thus, the account of Dunstan is pervaded by a prejudice which is the fruit of anything but knowledge; Edward the Confessor is "the dreary old" and "the maudlin Confessor;" and the Pope and what belongs to him are treated with a measure of contumely which would have satisfied the heart of Leigh Hunt himself. To be sure, if King John is dismissed as a "miserable brute," King Henry the Eighth is not more courteously designated as a "blot of blood and grease upon the history of England." On the other hand it could hardly be but that certain passages of the national story should be well told by so great a master of narrative; and though the strain in which parts of the history of Charles the Second are recounted strikes one as hardly suitable to the young, to whom irony is in general *caviare* indeed, yet there are touches both in the story of "this merry gentleman"—a designation which almost recalls Fagin—and elsewhere in the book not unworthy of its author. *Its* patriotic spirit

is quite as striking as its radicalism; and vulgar as some
of its expressions must be called, there is a pleasing glow
in the passage on King Alfred, which declares the
"English-Saxon" character to have been "the greatest
character among the nations of the earth;" and there
is a yet nobler enthusiasm, such as it would indeed be
worth any writer's while to infuse into the young, in the
passionate earnestness with which, by means of the story
of Agincourt, the truth is enforced that "nothing can
make war otherwise than horrible."

This book must have been dictated, and some at least
of the latter portion of *Bleak House* written, at Boulogne,
where, after a spring sojourn at Brighton, Dickens spent
the summer of 1853, and where were also passed the
summers of 1854 and 1856. Boulogne, where Le Sage's
last years were spent, was *Our French Watering-place*,
so graphically described in a paper in *Household Words*
as a companion picture to the old familiar Broadstairs.
The family were comfortably settled on a green hill-
side close to the town, "in a charming garden in a
very pleasant country," with "excellent light wines on
the premises, French cookery, millions of roses, two
cows—for milk-punch—vegetables cut for the pot, and
handed in at the kitchen window; five summer-houses,
fifteen fountains—with no water in 'em—and thirty-seven
clocks—keeping, as I conceive, Australian time, having no
reference whatever to the hours on this side of the globe."
The energetic owner of the Villa des Moulineaux was
the "M. Loyal Devasseur" of *Our French Watering-
place* — jovial, convivial, genial, sentimental too as a
Buonapartist and a patriot. In 1854 the same obliging
personage housed the Dickens family in another abode at
the top of the hill, close to the famous Napoleonic column;

but in 1856 they came back to the Moulineaux. The
former year had been an exciting one for Englishmen
in France, with royal visits to and fro to testify to the
entente cordiale between the governments. Dickens, notwithstanding his humorous assertions, was only moderately
touched by the Sebastopol fever; but when a concrete
problem came before him in the shape of a festive demon-
stration, he addressed himself to it with the irrepressible
ardour of the born stage-manager. " In our own proper
illumination," he writes on the occasion of the Prince
Consort's visit to the camp at Boulogne, " I laid on all the
servants, all the children now at home, all the visitors,
one to every window, with everything ready to light up
on the ringing of a big dinner-bell by your humble correspondent.   St. Peter's on Easter Monday was the
result."

Of course, at Boulogne, Dickens was cut off neither
from his business nor from his private friends. His
hospitable invitations were as urgent to his French villa
in the summer as to his London house in the winter,
and on both sides of the water the *Household Words*
familiars were as sure of a welcome from their chief.
During his absences from London he could have had
no trustier lieutenant than Mr. W. H. Wills, with
whom, being always ready to throw himself into a part,
he corresponded in an amusing paragraphed semi-official
style.   And neither in his working nor in his leisure
hours had he by this time any more cherished companion than Mr. Wilkie Collins, whose progress towards
brilliant success he was watching with the keenest
and kindliest interest.   With him and his old friend
Augustus Egg, Dickens, in October, 1853, started on a
tour to Switzerland and Italy, in the course of which

he saw more than one old friend, and revisited more than
one known scene—ascending Vesuvius with Mr. Layard
and drinking punch at Rome with David Roberts. It
would be absurd to make any lofty demands upon the
brief records of a holiday journey; and, for my part,
I would rather think of Dickens assiduous over his
Christmas number at Rome and at Venice, than weigh his
moralisings about the electric telegraph running through
the Coliseum. His letters written to his wife during this
trip are bright and gay, and it was certainly no roving
bachelor who "kissed almost all the children he encountered
in remembrance of the sweet faces" of his own, and "talked
to all the mothers who carried them." By the middle of
December the travellers were home again, and before
the year was out he had read to large audiences at Birmingham, on behalf of a public institution, his favourite
Christmas stories of the *Christmas Carol* and *The Cricket
on the Hearth.* As yet, however, his mind was not
seriously intent upon any labours but those proper to his
career as an author, and the year 1854 saw, between the
months of April and August, the publication in his
journal of a new story, which is among the most characteristic, though not among the most successful, of his
works of fiction.

In comparison with most of Dickens' novels, *Hard
Times* is contained within a narrow compass; and this with
the further necessity of securing to each successive small
portion of the story a certain immediate degree of effectiveness, accounts, in some measure, for the peculiarity of the
impression left by this story upon many of its readers.
Short as the story relatively is, few of Dickens' fictions
were elaborated with so much care. He had not intended
to write a new story for a twelvemonth, when, as he says,

importance of the principles which *Hard Times* was
intended to illustrate. Nor is it of much moment
whether the illustrations are always exact; whether the
"Commissioners of Facts" have reason to protest that
the unimaginative character of their processes does not
necessarily imply an unimaginative purpose in their ends;
whether there is any actual Coketown in existence within
a hundred miles of Manchester; or whether it suffices
that "everybody knew what was meant, but every
cotton-spinning town said it was the other cotton-spinning town." The chief personal grievance of Stephen
Blackpool has been removed or abated, but the "muddle"
is not yet altogether cleared up which prevents the nation
and the "national dustmen," its lawgivers, from impar-
tially and sympathetically furthering the interest of all
classes. In a word, the moral of *Hard Times* has not yet
lost its force, however imperfect or unfair the method
may have been in which it is urged in the book.

Unfortunately, however, a work of art with a didactic
purpose is only too often prone to exaggerate what seems
of special importance for the purpose in question, and to
heighten contrasts which seem likely to put it in the
clearest light. "Thomas Gradgrind, sir," who announces
himself with something of the genuine Lancashire roll,
and his system are a sound and a laughable piece of satire
to begin with, only here and there marred by the satirist's
imperfect knowledge of the details which he caricatures.
The "Manchester School," which the novel strives to
expose, is in itself to a great extent a figment of the
imagination, which to this day serves to round many
a hollow period in oratory and journalism. Who, it
may fairly be asked, were the parliamentary politicians
satirised in the member for Coketown, deaf and blind to

any consideration but the multiplication table. But in any case the cause hardly warrants one of its consequences as depicted in the novel—the utter brutalisation of a stolid nature like "the Whelp's." When Gradgrind's son is about to be shipped abroad out of reach of the penalties of his crime, he reminds his father that he merely exemplifies the statistical law that "so many people out of so many will be dishonest." When the virtuous Bitzer is indignantly asked whether he has a heart, he replies that he is physiologically assured of the fact; and to the further inquiry whether this heart of his is accessible to compassion, makes answer that "it is accessible to reason, and to nothing else." These returnings of Mr. Gradgrind's philosophy upon himself savour of the moral justice represented by Gratiano in the fourth act. So again, Coketown with its tall chimneys and black river, and its thirteen religious denominations, to which whoever else belonged the working men did *not*, is no perverse contradiction of fact. But the influence of Coketown, or of a whole wilderness of Coketowns, cannot justly be charged with a tendency to ripen such a product as Josiah Bounderby, who is not only the "bully of humanity," but proves to be a mean-spirited impostor in his pretensions to the glory of self-help. In short, *Hard Times* errs by its attempt to prove too much.

Apart, however, from the didactic purposes which overburden it, the pathos and humour of particular portions of this tale appear to me to have been in nowise overrated. The domestic tragedy of Stephen and Rachael has a subdued intensity of tenderness and melancholy of a kind rare with Dickens, upon whom the example of Mrs. Gaskell in this instance may not have been without

K

its influence. Nor is there anything more delicately and at the same time more appropriately conceived in any of his works, than poor Rachael's dominion over the imagination as well as over the affections of her noble-minded and unfortunate lover : " as the shining stars were to the heavy candle in the window, so was Rachael, in the rugged fancy of this man, to the common experiences of his life." The love-story of poor Louisa is of a different kind, and more wordy in the telling ; yet here also the feelings painted are natural and true. The humorous interest is almost entirely concentrated upon the company of horse-riders ; and never has Dickens' extraordinary power of humorous observation more genially asserted itself. From Mr. Sleary—" thtout man, game-eye "—and his protagonist, Mr. E. W. B. Childers, who, when he shook his long hair, caused it to "shake all at once," down to Master Kidderminster, who used to form the apex of the human pyramids, and "in whose young nature there was an original flavour of the misanthrope," these honest equestrians are more than worthy to stand by the side of Mr. Vincent Crummles and his company of actors ; and the fun has here, in addition to the grotesqueness of the earlier picture, a mellowness of its own. Dickens' comic genius was never so much at its ease and so inexhaustible in ludicrous fancies, as in the depiction of such groups as this ; and the horse-riders, skilfully introduced to illustrate a truth, wholesome if not novel, would have insured popularity so a far less interesting, and to a far less powerful fiction.

The year after that which saw the publication of *Hard Times* was one in which the thoughts of most Englishmen were turned away from the problems approached in that story. But if the military glories of 1854 had not aroused

in him any very exuberant enthusiasm, the reports from the
Crimea in the ensuing winter were more likely to appeal
to his patriotism as well as to his innate impatience of
disorder and incompetence. In the first instance, however,
he contented himself with those grumblings to which, as
a sworn foe of red tape and a declared disbeliever in our
Parliamentary system, he might claim to have a special
right; and he seems to have been too restless in and about
himself to have entered very closely into the progress of
public affairs. The Christmas had been a merry one at
Tavistock House; and the amateur theatricals of its
juvenile company had passed through a most successful
season. Their history has been written by one of the
performers—himself not the least distinguished of the
company, since it was he who, in Dickens' house,
caused Thackeray to roll off his seat in a fit of
laughter. Dickens, who with Mark Lemon disported
himself among these precocious minnows, was, as our
chronicler relates, like Triplet, "author, manager, and
actor too," organiser, deviser, and harmoniser of all the
incongruous assembled elements; it was he "who impro-
vised costumes, painted and corked our innocent cheeks,
and suggested all the most effective business of the scene."
But as was usual with him, the transition was rapid from
play to something very like earnest; and already in June,
1855, the Tavistock House theatre produced Mr. Wilkie
Collins' melodrama of *The Lighthouse*, which afterwards
found its way to the public stage. To Dickens, who performed in it with the author, it afforded " scope for a piece
of acting of great power," the old sailor Aaron Gurnock,
which by its savage picturesqueness earned a tribute of
recognition from Carlyle. No less a hand than Stanfield painted the scenery, and Dickens himself, besides

direction of the navy—than in every other branch of the
public service put together, including "—the particularisa-
tion is hard—" even the Woods and Forests." He had
listened, we may be sure, to the scornful denunciations
launched by the prophet of the *Latter-Day Pamphlets*
against Downing Street and all its works, and to the
proclamation of the great though rather vague truth that
"reform in that Downing Street department of affairs is
precisely the reform which were worth all others." And
now the heartrending sufferings of multitudes of brave
men had brought to light, in one department of the public
administration, a series of complications and perversities
which in the end became so patent to the Government
itself, that they had to be roughly remedied in the very
midst of the struggle. The cry for administrative reform,
which arose in the year 1855, however crude the form it
frequently took, was in itself a logical enough result of
the situation ; and there is no doubt that the angriness of
the complaint was intensified by the attitude taken up in
the House of Commons by the head of the Government
towards the pertinacious politician who made himself the
mouthpiece of the extreme demands of the feeling outside.
Mr. Layard was Dickens' valued friend ; and the share
is thus easily explained, which—against his otherwise
uniform practice of abstaining from public meetings—the
most popular writer of the day took in the Administrative
Reform meetings, held in Drury Lane Theatre, on June
27th, 1855. The speech which he delivered on this
occasion, and which was intended to aid in forcing the
"whole question" of Administrative Reform upon the
attention of an unwilling Government, possesses no value
whatever in connexion with its theme, though of course
it is not devoid of some smart and telling hits. Not on

the platform, but at his desk as an author, was Dickens
to do real service to the cause of administrative efficiency.
For while invective of a general kind runs off like water
from the rock of usage, even Circumlocution Offices are
not insensible to the acetous force of satire.

Dickens' caricature of British officialism formed the
most generally attractive element in the story of *Little
Dorrit*—originally intended to be called *Nobody's Fault*
—which he published in monthly numbers, from December, 1855, to June, 1857. He was solemnly taken
to task for his audacity by the *Edinburgh Review*, which
reproached him for his persistent ridicule of "the institutions of the country, the laws, the administration,
in a word, the government under which we live."
His "charges" were treated as hardly seriously meant,
but as worthy of severe reprobation because likely to be
seriously taken by the poor, the uneducated, and the
young. And the caricaturist, besides being reminded
of the names of several eminent public servants, was
specially requested to look, as upon a picture contrasting
with his imaginary Circumlocution Office, upon the Post
Office, or, for the choice offered was not more extensive,
upon the London police so liberally praised by himself in
his own journal. The delighted author of *Little Dorrit*
replied to this not very skilful diatribe in a short and
spirited rejoinder in *Household Words*. In this he
judiciously confined himself to refuting an unfounded
incidental accusation in the Edinburgh article, and to
dwelling, as upon a "Curious Misprint," upon the indignant query : "How does he account for the career of
Mr. Rowland Hill?" whose name, as an example of the
ready intelligence of the Circumlocution Office, was
certainly an odd *erratum.* Had he, however, cared to

make a more general reply to the main article of the
indictment, he might have pointed out that, as a matter
of fact, our official administrative machinery *had* recently
broken down in one of its most important branches, and
that circumlocution in the literal sense of the word—
circumlocution between department and department, or
office and office—had been one of the principal causes
of the collapse. The general drift of the satire was
therefore, in accordance with fact, and the satire itself
salutary in its character. To quarrel with it for not
taking into consideration what might be said on the other
side, was to quarrel with the method of treatment which
satire has at all times considered itself entitled to adopt ;
while to stigmatise a popular book as likely to mislead
the ill-informed, was to suggest a restraint which would
have deprived wit and humour of most of their opportunities of rendering service to either a good or an evil
cause.

A far more legitimate exception has been taken to these
Circumlocution Office episodes as defective in art by the
very reason of their being exaggerations. Those best
acquainted with the interiors of our government offices
may be right in denying that the Barnacles can be
regarded as an existing type. Indeed, it would at no
time have been easy to point to any office quite as
labyrinthine, or quite as bottomless, as that permanently
presided over by Mr. Tite Barnacle; to any chief secretary
or commissioner so absolutely wooden of fibre as he ; or
to any private secretary so completely absorbed in his
eyeglass as Barnacle junior. But as satirical figures they
one and all fulfil their purpose, as thoroughly as the
picture of the official sanctum itself with its furniture
"in the higher official manner," and its "general bam-

boozling air of how not to do it." The only question is, whether satire which, if it is to be effective, must be of a piece and in its way exaggerated, is not out of place in a pathetic and humorous fiction, where, like a patch of too diverse a thread, it interferes with the texture into which it is introduced. In themselves these passages of *Little Dorrit* deserve to remain unforgotten among the masterpieces of literary caricature ; and there is, I do not hesitate to say, something of Swiftian force in their grotesque embodiment of a popular current of indignation. The mere name of the Circumlocution Office was a stroke of genius, one of those phrases of Dickens which Professor Masson justly describes as, whether exaggerated or not, " efficacious for social reform." As usual, Dickens had made himself well acquainted with the formal or outside part of his subject ; the very air of Whitehall seems to gather round us as Mr. Tite Barnacle, in answer to a persistent inquirer who "wants to know" the position of a particular matter, concedes that it " may have been, in the course of official business, referred to the Circumlocution Office for its consideration," and that "the department may have either originated, or confirmed, a minute on the subject." In the *Household Words* paper, called *A Poor Man's Tale of a Patent* (1850), will be found a sufficiently elaborate study for Mr. Doyce's experiences of the government of his country, as wrathfully narrated by Mr. Meagles.

With the exception of the Circumlocution Office passages, —adventitious as they are to the progress of the action, *Little Dorrit* exhibits a palpable falling-off in inventive power. Forster illustrates by a striking facsimile the difference between the " labour and pains " of the author's short notes for *Little Dorrit* and the " lightness and confidence of handling" in what hints he had jotted down for *David Copperfield*. Indeed, his "tablets" had about this time begun to be an essential part of his literary equipment. But in *Little Dorrit* there are enough internal signs of, possibly unconscious, lassitude. The earlier, no doubt, is, in every respect, the better part of the book; or, rather, the later part shows the author wearily at work upon a canvas too wide for him, and filling it up with a crowd of personages in whom it is difficult to take much interest. Even Mr. Merdle and his catastrophe produce the effect rather of a ghastly allegory than of an "extravagant conception," as the author ironically called it in his preface, derived only too directly from real life. In the earlier part of the book, in so far as it is not once again concerned with enforcing the moral of *Hard Times* in a different way, by means of Mrs. Clennam and her son's early history, the humour of Dickens plays freely over the figure of the Father of the Marshalsea. It is a psychological masterpiece in its way; but the revolting selfishness of Little Dorrit's father is not redeemed artistically by her own longsuffering; for her pathos lacks the old irresistible ring. Doubtless much in this part of the story—the whole episode, for instance, of the honest turnkey—is in the author's best manner. But admirable as it is, this new picture of prison-life and prison-sentiment has an undercurrent of bitterness, indeed, almost of contemptuousness, foreign to the best part of Dickens' genius. This is still more perceptible in a figure not less true to life than the Father of the Marshalsea himself—Flora, the overblown flower of Arthur Clennam's boyish love. The humour of the conception is undeniable, but the whole effect is cruel; and, though greatly amused, the reader feels almost as if he were abetting a profanation. Dickens

could not have become what he is to the great multitude
of his readers had he, as a humorist, often indulged in
this cynical mood.

There is in general little in the characters of this fiction
to compensate for the sense of oppression from which, as
he follows the slow course of its far from striking plot,
the reader finds it difficult to free himself. A vein of genuine
humour shows itself in Mr. Plornish, obviously a favourite
of the author's, and one of those genuine working men, as
rare in fiction as on the stage, where Mr. Toole has reproduced the species; but the relation between Mr. and Mrs.
Plornish is only a fainter revival of that between Mr.
and Mrs. Bagnet.   Nor is there anything fresh or novel
in the characters belonging to another social sphere.
Henry Gowan, apparently intended as an elaborate study
in psychology, is only a very tedious one; and his
mother at Hampton Court, whatever phase of a dilapi-
dated aristocracy she may be intended to caricature, is
merely illbred.   As for Mrs. General, she is so sorry a
burlesque that she could not be reproduced without
extreme caution even on the stage—to the reckless conven-
tionalities of which, indeed, the whole picture of the Dorrit
family as *nouveaux riches* bears a striking resemblance.
There is, on the contrary, some good caricature, which, in
one instance at least, was thought transparent by the
knowing, in the *silhouettes* of the great Mr. Merdle's professional guests; but these are, like the Circumlocution
Office puppets, satiric sketches, not the living figures of
creative humour.

I have spoken of this story with a censure which may
be regarded as exaggerated in its turn.   But I well remember, at the time of its publication in numbers, the general
consciousness that *Little Dorrit* was proving unequal to the

high-strung expectations which a new work by Dickens then
excited in his admirers both young and old. There were
new and striking features in it, with abundant comic and
serious effect, but there was no power in the whole story
to seize and hold, and the feeling could not be escaped that
the author was not at his best. And Dickens was not at
his best when he wrote *Little Dorrit*. Yet while nothing
is more remarkable in the literary career of Dickens than
this apparently speedy decline of his power, nothing is
more wonderful in it than the degree to which he righted
himself again, not, indeed, with his public, for the public
never deserted its favourite, but with his genius.

A considerable part of *Little Dorrit* must have been
written in Paris ; where, in October, after a quiet autumn
at Folkestone, Dickens had taken a family apartment
in the Avenue des Champs Élysées, "about half a quarter
of a mile above Franconi's." Here, after his fashion, he
lived much to himself, his family and his guests, only
occasionally finding his way into a literary or artistic
salon ; but he sat for his portrait to both Ary and Henri
Scheffer, and was easily persuaded to read his *Cricket on
the Hearth* to an audience in the atelier. Macready and
Mr. Wilkie Collins were in turn the companions of many
"theatrical and lounging" evenings. Intent as Dickens
now had become upon the technicalities of his own form
of composition, this interest must have been greatly stimulated by the frequent comparison of modern French plays,
in most of which nicety of construction and effectiveness
of situation have so paramount a significance. At Boulogne, too, Mr. Wilkie Collins was a welcome summer
visitor. And in the autumn the two friends started on
the *Lazy Tour of Two Idle Apprentices*. It came to an
untimely end as a pedestrian excursion, but the record of

it is one of the pleasantest memorials of a friendship
which brightened much of Dickens' life and intensified
his activity in work as well as in pleasure.

"Mr. Thomas Idle" had indeed a busy time of it in
this year 1857.   The publication of *Little Dorrit* was not
finished till June, and in August we find him, between a
reading and a performance of *The Frozen Deep* at Manchester—then in the exciting days of the great Art Exhibi-
tion—thus describing to Macready his way of filling up his
time : "I hope you have seen my tussle with the *Edinburgh*.
I saw the chance last Friday week, as I was going down to
read the *Carol* in St. Martin's Hall.   Instantly turned to,
then and there, and wrote half the article, flew out of bed
early next morning, and finished it by noon.   Went down
to Gallery of Illustration (we acted that night), did the
day's business, corrected the proofs in Polar costume in
dressing-room, broke up two numbers of *Household Words*
to get it out directly, played in *Frozen Deep* and *Uncle
John*, presided at supper of company, made no end of
speeches, went home and gave in completely for four hours,
then got sound asleep, and next day was as fresh as you
used to be in the far-off days of your lusty youth."   It
was on the occasion of the readings at St. Martin's Hall,
for the benefit of Douglas Jerrold's family, that the thought
of giving readings for his own benefit first suggested
itself to Dickens ; and, as will be seen, by April, 1858, the
idea had been carried into execution, and a new phase of
life had begun for him.   And yet at this very time, when
his home was about to cease being in the fullest sense a
home to Dickens, by a strange irony of fortune, he had
been enabled to carry out a long-cherished fancy and to
take possession, in the first instance as a summer residence,
of the house on Gad's Hill, of which a lucky chance had

made him the owner rather more than a twelvemonth before.

"My little place," he wrote in 1858, to his Swiss friend Cerjat, "is a grave red-brick house (time of George the First, I suppose), which I have added to and stuck bits upon in all manner of ways, so that it is as pleasantly irregular, and as violently opposed to all architectural ideas, as the most hopeful man could possibly desire. It is on the summit of Gad's Hill. The robbery was committed before the door, on the man with the treasure, and Falstaff ran away from the identical spot of ground now covered by the room in which I write. A little rustic alehouse, called 'The Sir John Falstaff,' is over the way—has been over the way ever since, in honour of the event. . . . The whole stupendous property is on the old Dover road. . . ."

Among "the blessed woods and fields" which, as he says, had done him "a world of good," in a season of unceasing bodily and mental unrest, the great English writer had indeed found a habitation fitted to become inseparable from his name and fame. It was not till rather later, in 1860, that, after the sale of Tavistock House, Gad's Hill Place became his regular abode, a London house being only now and then taken for the season, while furnished rooms were kept at the office in Wellington Street for occasional use. And it was only gradually that he enlarged and improved his Kentish place so as to make it the pretty and comfortable country-house which at the present day it appears to be; constructing, in course of time, the passage under the highroad to the shrubbery, where the Swiss châlet given to him by Mr. Fechter was set up, and building the pretty little conservatory, which, when completed, he was not to live many days to enjoy. But an old-fashioned homely look, free from the slightest affectation of quietness, belonged to Gad's Hill Place, even after all these alterations, and belongs to it even at this day, when Dickens' solid old-fashioned furniture has been changed. In the pretty little front hall still hangs the illuminated tablet recalling the legend of Gad's Hill; and on the inside panels of the library door remain the facetious sham book-titles: "Hudson's *Complete Failure*," and "*Ten Minutes in China*," and "Cats' *Lives*," and, on a long series of leather backs, "Hansard's *Guide to Refreshing Sleep*." The rooms are all of a modest size, and the bed-rooms—among them Dickens' own—very low; but the whole house looks thoroughly habitable, while the views across the cornfields at the back are such as in their undulation of soft outline are nowhere more pleasant than in Kent. Rochester and the Medway are near, even for those who do not—like Dickens and his dogs—count a stretch past three or four "milestones on the Dover road" as the mere beginning of an afternoon's walk. At a distance little greater there are in one direction the green glades of Cobham Park, with Chalk and Gravesend beyond; and in another the flat country towards the Thames, with its abundance of market-gardens. There, too, are the marshes on the border of which lie the massive ruin of Cooling Castle, the refuge of the Lollard martyr who was *not* concerned in the affair on Gad's Hill, and Cooling Church and churchyard, with the quaint little gravestones in the grass. London and the office were within easy reach, and Paris itself was, for practical purposes, not much farther away, so that, in later days at all events, Dickens found himself "crossing the Channel perpetually."

The name of Dickens still has a good sound in and about Gad's Hill. He was on very friendly terms with

some families whose houses stand near to his own; and
though nothing was farther from his nature, as he says,
than to "wear topboots" and play the squire, yet he had
in him not a little of what endears so many a resident
country gentleman to his neighbourhood.   He was
head organiser rather than chief patron of village sports,
of cricket matches and foot races; and his house was
a dispensary for the poor of the parish.   He established confidential relations between his house and the
Falstaff Inn over the way, regulating his servants' con-
sumption of beer on a strict but liberal plan of his own
devising; but it is not for this reason only that the
successor of Mr. Edwin Trood—for such was the veritable
name of mine host of the Falstaff in Dickens' time—
declares that it was a bad day for the neighbourhood
when Dickens was taken away from it.   In return,
nothing could exceed the enthusiasm which surrounded
him in his own country, and Forster has described his
astonishment at the manifestation of it on the occasion of
the wedding of the youngest daughter of the house in
1860.   And, indeed, he was born to be popular, and
specially among those by whom he was beloved as a
friend or honoured as a benefactor.

But it was not for long intervals of either work or
rest that Dickens was to settle down in his pleasant
country house, nor was he ever, except quite at the last,
to sit down under his own roof in peace and quiet, a
wanderer no more.   Less than a year after he had taken
up his residence for the summer on Gad's Hill, his home,
and that of his younger children, was his wife's home
no longer.   The separation, which appears to have been
preparing itself for some, but no very long, time, took
place in May, 1858, when, after an amicable arrange-

ment, Mrs. Dickens left her husband, who henceforth
allowed her an ample separate maintenance, and occasionally corresponded with her, but never saw her again.   The
younger children remained in their father's house under the
self-sacrificing and devoted care of Mrs. Dickens' surviving
sister, Miss Hogarth. Shortly afterwards, Dickens thought
it well, in printed words which may be left forgotten, to
rebut some slanderous gossip which, as the way of the
world is, had misrepresented the circumstances of this
separation.   The causes of the event were an open secret
to his friends and acquaintances.   If he had ever loved
his wife with that affection before which so-called incom-
patibilities of habits, temper, or disposition fade into
nothingness, there is no indication of it in any of his
numerous letters addressed to her.   Neither has it ever
been pretended that he strove in the direction of that
resignation which love and duty together made possible
to David Copperfield, or even that he remained in every
way master of himself, as many men have known how to
remain, the story of whose wedded life and its disappointments has never been written in history or figured in
fiction.   It was not incumbent upon his faithful friend
and biographer, and much less can it be upon one whom
nothing but a sincere admiration of Dickens' genius
entitles to speak of him at all, to declare the standard by
which the most painful transaction in his life is to be
judged. I say the most painful, for it is with a feeling akin
to satisfaction that one reads, in a letter three years afterwards to a lady in reference to her daughter's wedding :
"I want to thank you also for thinking of me on the
occasion, but I feel that I am better away from it.   I
should really have a misgiving that I was a sort of a
shadow on a young marriage, and you will understand

capricious extravagances of a Balzac or a Dumas, nor can
he have been at a loss how to make due provision for
those whom in the course of nature he would leave behind
him.   Love of money for its own sake, or for that of the
futilities it can purchase, was altogether foreign to his
nature.   At the same time, the rapid making of large
sums has potent attractions for most men ; and these
attractions are perhaps strongest for those who engage in
the pursuit for the sake of the race as well as of the prize.
Dickens' readings were virtually something new ; their
success was not only all his own, but unique and unprecedented, what nobody but himself ever had achieved or
ever could have achieved.   Yet the determining motive—
if I read his nature rightly—was after all of another kind.
"Two souls dwelt in his breast ;" and when their aspira-
tions united in one appeal it was irresistible.   The author
who craved for the visible signs of a sympathy responding
to that which he felt for his multitudes of readers, and the
actor who longed to impersonate creations already beings
of flesh and blood to himself, were both astir in him, and
in both capacities he felt himself drawn into the very
publicity deprecated by his friends.   He liked, as one
who knew him thoroughly said to me, to be face to face
with his public ; and against this liking, which he had
already indulged as fully as he could without passing the
boundaries between private and professional life, arguments were in vain.   It has been declared sheer pedantry
to speak of such boundaries ; and to suggest that there is
anything degrading in paid readings such as those of
Dickens would, on the face of it, be absurd.   On the
other hand, the author who, on or off the stage, becomes
the interpreter of his writings to large audiences, more
especially if he does his best to stereotype his interpretation

by constantly repeating it, limits his own prerogative of
being many things to many men; and where the author
of a work, more particularly of a work of fiction, adjusts
it to circumstances differing from those of its production,
he allows the requirements of the lesser art to prejudice
the claims of the greater.

Dickens cannot have been blind to these considera-
tions; but to others his eyes were never opened. He
found much that was inspiriting in his success as a
reader, and this not only in the large sums he gained,
or even in the "roaring sea of response," to use his
own fine metaphor, of which he had become accustomed to "stand upon the beach." His truest sentiment as an author was touched to the quick; and he
was, as he says himself, "brought very near to what he
had sometimes dreamed might be his fame," when at
York, a lady, whose face he had never seen, stopped him
in the street, and said to him: "Mr. Dickens, will you let
me touch the hand that has filled my house with many
friends?" or when at Belfast, he was almost overwhelmed
with entreaties "to shake hands, Misther Dickens, and
God bless you, sir; not ounly for the light you've been
to me this night, but for the light you've been in
mee house, sir—and God love your face!—this many a
year." On the other hand—and this, perhaps, a nature
like his would not be the quickest to perceive—there
was something vulgarising in the constant striving after
immediate success, in the shape of large audiences, loud
applause, and satisfactory receipts. The conditions of the
actor's art cannot forego these stimulants; and this is
precisely his disadvantage in comparison with artists who
are able to possess themselves in quiet. To me, at least,
it is painful to find Dickens jubilantly recording how at

Dublin " eleven bank-notes were thrust into the pay-box
—Arthur saw them—at one time for eleven stalls ; " how
at Edinburgh, " neither Grisi, nor Jenny Lind, nor anything, nor anybody, seems to make the least effect on the
draw of the readings ; " while, every allowance being
made, there is something almost ludicrous in the double
assertion, that " the most delicate audience I had ever
seen in any provincial place is Canterbury ; but the
audience with the greatest sense of humour, certainly is
Dover." What subjects for parody Dickens would have
found in these innocent ecstasies if uttered by any other
man ! Undoubtedly, this enthusiasm was closely connected with the very thoroughness with which he entered
into the work of his readings. " You have no idea," he
tells Forster, in 1867, " how I have worked at them.
Finding it necessary, as their reputation widened, that
they should be better than at first, *I have learnt them all,*
so as to have no mechanical drawback in looking after the
words. I have tested all the serious passion in them by
everything I know ; made the humorous points much more
humorous ; corrected my utterance of certain words ; cultivated a self-possession not to be disturbed ; and made
myself master of the situation." " From ten years ago to
last night," he writes to his son from Baltimore in 1868,
" I have never read to an audience but I have watched
for an opportunity of striking out something better some-
where." The freshness with which he returned night
after night and season after season, to the sphere of his
previous successes, was itself a genuine actor's gift ; " so
real," he declares, " are my fictions to myself, that, after
hundreds of nights, I come with a feeling of perfect
freshness to that little red table, and laugh and cry with
my hearers as if I had never stood there before."

Dickens' first public readings were given at Birmingham, during the Christmas week of 1853–54, in support of the new Midland Institute; but a record—for the authenticity of which I cannot vouch—remains, that with true theatrical instinct he, before the Christmas in question, gave a trial reading of the *Christmas Carol* to a smaller public audience at Peterborough. He had since been repeatedly found willing to read for benevolent purposes; and the very fact that it had become necessary to decline some of these frequent invitations, had again suggested the possibility—which had occurred to him eleven years before—of meeting the demand in a different way. Yet it may, after all, be doubted whether the idea of undertaking an entire series of paid public readings would have been carried out, had it not been for the general restlessness which had seized upon Dickens early in 1858, when, moreover, he had no special task either of labour or of leisure to absorb him, and when he craved for excitement more than ever. To go home —in this springtime of 1858—was not to find there the peace of contentment. " I must do *something*," he wrote in March to his faithful counsellor, " or I shall wear my heart away. I can see no better thing to do that is half so hopeful in itself, or half so well suited to my restless state."

So by April the die was cast, and on the 29th of that month he had entered into his new relation with the public. One of the strongest and most genuine impulses of his nature had victoriously asserted itself, and according to his wont he addressed himself to his task with a relentless vigour which flinched from no exertion. He began with a brief series at St. Martin's Hall, and then, his invaluable friend Arthur Smith continuing to act as his manager, he contrived to cram not less than eighty-seven readings into three months and a half of travelling in the "provinces," including Scotland and Ireland. A few winter readings in London, and a short supplementary course in the country during October, 1859, completed this first series. Already, in 1858, we find him, in a letter from Ireland, complaining of the "tremendous strain," and declaring, "I seem to be always either in a railway carriage, or reading, or going to bed. I get so knocked up, whenever I have a minute to remember it, that then I go to bed as a matter of course." But the enthusiasm which everywhere welcomed him—I can testify to the thrill of excitement produced by his visit to Cambridge, in October, 1859—repaid him for his fatigues. Scotland thawed to him, and with Dublin—where his success was extraordinary—he was so smitten, as to think it at first sight "pretty nigh as big as Paris." In return, the Boots at Morrison's expressed the general feeling in a patriotic point of view : "Whaat sart of a hoose, sur ?" he asked me. "Capital." "The Lard be praised, for the 'onor o' Dooblin !"

The books, or portions of books, to which he confined himself during this first series of readings, were few in number. They comprised the *Carol* and the *Chimes*, and two stories from earlier Christmas numbers of *Household Words*—may the exclamation of the soft-hearted chambermaid at the Holly Tree Inn, "It's a shame to part 'em !" never vanish from my memory!—together with the episodic readings of the *Trial* in *Pickwick*, *Mrs. Gamp*, and *Paul Dombey*. Of these the *Pickwick*, which I heard more than once, is still vividly present to me. The only drawback to the complete enjoyment of it was the lurking fear that there had been some tampering with the text, not to be condoned even in its author. But in the way of assumption, Charles Mathews the elder himself could have accomplished no more Protean effort. The lacklustre eye of Mr. Justice Stareleigh, the forensic hitch of Mr. Serjeant Buzfuz, and the hopeless impotence of Mr. Nathaniel Winkle, were alike incomparable. And if the success of the impersonation of Mr. Samuel Weller was less complete—although Dickens had formerly acted the character on an amateur stage—the reason probably was that, by reason of his endless store of ancient and modern instances, Sam had himself become a quasi-mythical being, whom it was almost painful to find reproduced in flesh and blood.

I have not hesitated to treat these readings by Dickens as if they had been the performances of an actor; and the description would apply even more strongly to his later readings, in which he seemed to make his points in a more accentuated fashion than before. "His readings," says Mr. C. Kent, in an interesting little book about them, "were, in the fullest meaning of the words, singularly ingenious and highly-elaborated histrionic performances." As such, they had been prepared with a care such as few actors bestow upon their parts, and—for the book was prepared not less than the reading—not all authors bestow upon their plays. Now the art of reading, even in the case of dramatic works, has its own laws, which even the most brilliant readers cannot neglect except at their peril. A proper pitch has to be found in the first instance, before the exceptional passages can be, as it were, marked off from it; and the absence of this groundtone sometimes interfered with the total effect of a reading by Dickens. On the other hand, the exceptional passages were, if not uniformly, at least generally excellent; nor am I at all disposed to agree with Forster in preferring, as a rule, the humorous to the pathetic. At the same time, there was noticeable in these readings a certain hardness which competent critics likewise discerned in Dickens' acting, and which could not, at least in the former case, be regarded as an ordinary characteristic of dilettanteism. The truth is that he isolated his parts too sharply—a frequent fault of English acting, and one more detrimental to the total effect of a reading than even to that of an acted play.

No sooner had the heaviest stress of the first series of readings ceased, than Dickens was once more at work upon a new fiction. The more immediate purpose was to ensure a prosperous launch to the journal which, in the spring of 1859, took the place of *Household Words*. A dispute, painful in its origin, but ending in an amicable issue, had resulted in the purchase of that journal by Dickens; but already a little earlier, he had—as he was entitled to do—begun the new venture of *All the Year Round*, with which *Household Words* was afterwards incorporated. The first number, published on April 30th, contained the earliest instalment of *A Tale of Two Cities*, which was completed by November 20th following.

This story holds a unique place among the fictions of its author. Perhaps the most striking difference between it and his other novels may seem to lie in the all but entire absence from it of any humour or attempt at humour; for neither the brutalities of that "honest tradesman," Jerry, nor the laconisms of Miss Pross, can well be called by that name. Not that his sources of humour were drying up, even though, about this time, he contributed to an American journal a short "romance of the real world," *Hunted Down*, from which the same relief is again conspicuously absent. For the humour of Dickens was to assert itself with unmistakeable force in his next longer fiction, and was even before that, in some of his occasional papers, to give delightful proofs of its continued vigour. In the case of the *Tale of Two Cities*, he had a new and distinct design in his mind which did not indeed exclude humour, but with which a liberal indulgence in it must have seriously inter-fered. "I set myself," he writes, "the little task of writing a picturesque story, rising in every chapter with characters true to nature, but whom the story itself should express more than they should express themselves by dialogue. I mean, in other words, that I fancied a story of incident might be written, in place of the bestiality that is written under that pretence, pounding the characters out in its own mortar, and beating their own interests out of them." He therefore renounced his more usual method in favour of one probably less congenial to him. Yet, in his own opinion at least, he succeeded so well in the undertaking, that when the story was near its end, he could venture to express a hope that it was " the best story he had written." So much praise will hardly be given to this novel even by admirers of the French art of telling a story succinctly, or by those who can never resist a rather hysterical treatment of the French Revolution.

In my own opinion, *A Tale of Two Cities* is a skilfully though not perfectly constructed novel, which needed but little substantial alteration in order to be converted into a not less effective stage-play. And with such a design, Dickens actually sent the proof-sheets of the book to his friend Regnier, in the fearful hope that he might approve of the project of its dramatisation for a French theatre. Cleverly or clumsily adapted, the tale of the Revolution and its sanguinary vengeance was unlikely to commend itself to the Imperial censorship ; but an English version

was, I believe, afterwards very fairly successful on the
boards of the Adelphi, where Madame Celeste was certainly
in her right place as Madame Defarge, an excellent character for a melodrama, though rather wearisome as she
lies in wait through half a novel.

The construction of this story is, as I have said, skilful
but not perfect. Dickens himself successfully defended
his use of accident in bringing about the death of Madame
Defarge; the real objection to the conduct of this episode,
however, lies in the inadequacy of the contrivance for
leaving Miss Pross behind in Paris. Too much is also, I
think, made to turn upon the three words "and their
descendants"—non-essential in the original connexion—
by which Dr. Manette's written denunciation becomes
fatal to those he loves. Still, the general edifice
of the plot is solid; its interest is, notwithstanding
the crowded background, concentrated with much
skill upon a small group of personages; and Carton's
self-sacrifice, admirably prepared from the very first, pro-
duces a legitimate tragic effect. At the same time, the
novelist's art vindicates its own claims. Not only does
this story contain several narrative episodes of remarkable
power—such as the flight from Paris at the close, and the
touching little incident of the seamstress, told in Dickens'
sweetest pathetic manner—but it is likewise enriched
by some descriptive pictures of unusual excellence: for
instance, the sketch of Dover in the good old smuggling
times, and the mezzotint of the stormy evening in Soho.
Doubtless the increased mannerism of the style is disturbing, and this not only in the high-strung French
scenes. As to the historical element in this novel, Dickens
modestly avowed his wish that he might by his story
have been able "to add something to the popular and

picturesque means of understanding that terrible time, though no one can hope to add anything to Mr. Carlyle's wonderful book." But if Dickens desired to depict the noble of the *ancien régime*, either according to Carlyle or according to intrinsic probability, he should not have offered, in his Marquis, a type historically questionable, and unnatural besides. The description of the Saint Antoine, before and during the bursting of the storm, has in it more of truthfulness, or of the semblance of truthfulness ; and Dickens' perception of the physiognomy of the French workman is, I think, remarkably accurate. Altogether, the book is an extraordinary *tour de force*, which Dickens never repeated.

The opening of a new story by Dickens gave the necessary *impetus* to his new journal at its earliest stage ; nor was the ground thus gained ever lost. Mr. W. H. Wills stood by his chief's side as of old, taking, more especially in later years, no small share of responsibility upon him. The prospectus of *All the Year Round* had not in vain promised an identity of principle in its conduct with that of its predecessor ; in energy and spirit it showed no falling off ; and, though not in all respects, the personality of Dickens made itself felt as distinctly as ever. Besides the *Tale of Two Cities*, he contributed to it his story of *Great Expectations*. Among his contributors, Mr. Wilkie Collins took away the breath of multitudes of readers ; Mr. Charles Reade disported himself among the facts which gave stamina to his fiction ; and Lord Lytton made a daring voyage into a mysterious country. Thither Dickens followed him, for once, in his *Four Stories*, not otherwise noteworthy, and written in a manner already difficult to discriminate from that of Mr. Wilkie Collins. For the rest, the advice with which Dickens aided Lord

Lytton's progress in his *Strange Story* was neither more ready nor more painstaking than that which he bestowed upon his younger contributors, to more than one of whom he generously gave the opportunity of publishing in his journal a long work of fiction. Some of these younger writers were at this period among his most frequent guests and associates; for nothing more naturally commended itself to him than the encouragement of the younger generation.

But though longer imaginative works played at least as conspicuous a part in the new journal as they had in the old, the conductor likewise continued to make manifest his intention that the lesser contributions should not be treated by readers or by writers as harmless necessary "padding." For this purpose it was requisite not only that the choice of subjects should be made with the utmost care, but also that the master's hand should itself be occasionally visible. Dickens' occasional contributions had been few and unimportant, till in a happy hour he began a series of papers, including many of the pleasantest, as well as of the mellowest, among the lighter productions of his pen. As usual, he had taken care to find for this series a name which of itself went far to make its fortune.

I am both a town and a country traveller, and am always on the road. Figuratively speaking, I travel for the great house of Human Interest Brothers, and have rather a large connexion in the fancy goods way. Literally speaking, I am always wandering here and there from my rooms in Covent Garden, London—now about the city streets, now about the country byroads, seeing many little things and some great things, which, because they interest me, I think may interest others.

The whole collection of these *Uncommercial Traveller*

papers, together with the *Uncommercial Samples* which succeeded them after Dickens' return from America, and which begin with a graphic account of his homeward voyage *Aboard Ship*, where the voice of conscience spoke in the motion of the screw, amounts to thirty-seven articles, and spreads over a period of nine years. They are necessarily of varying merit, but among them are some which deserve a permanent place in our lighter literature. Such are the description of the churchyards on a quiet evening in *The City of the Absent*, the grotesque picture of loneliness in *Chambers*—a favourite theme with Dickens—and the admirable papers on *Shy Neighbourhoods* and on *Tramps*. Others have a biographical interest, though delightfully objective in treatment; yet others are mere fugitive pieces; but there are few without some of the most attractive qualities of Dickens' easiest style.

Dickens contributed other occasional papers to his journal, some of which may be forgotten without injury to his fame. Among these may be reckoned the rather dreary *George Silverman's Explanation* (1868), in which there is nothing characteristic but a vivid picture of a set of ranters, led by a clique of scoundrels; on the other hand, there will always be admirers of the pretty *Holiday Romance*, published nearly simultaneously in America and England, a nosegay of tales told by children, the only fault of which is that, as with other children's nosegays, there is perhaps a little too much of it. I have no room for helping to rescue from partial oblivion an old friend, whose portrait has not, I think, found a home among his master's collected sketches. Pincher's counterfeit has gone astray like *Pincher* himself. Meanwhile, the special institution of the Christmas Number flourished in connexion with *All the Year*

tributed by him to the Christmas Numbers, in addition to
these introductions, he at times gave the rein to his love
for the fanciful and the grotesque, which there was here
no reason to keep under. On the whole, written as in a
sense these compositions were to order, nothing is more
astonishing in them than his continued freshness, against
which his mannerism is here of vanishing importance;
and, inasmuch as after issuing a last Christmas Number of
a different kind, Dickens abandoned the custom when it
had reached the height of popular favour, and when
manifold imitations had offered him the homage of their
flattery, he may be said to have withdrawn from this
campaign in his literary life with banners flying.

In the year 1859 Dickens' readings had been comparatively few; and they had ceased altogether in the following year, when the *Uncommercial Traveller* began his
wanderings. The winter from 1859 to 1860 was his last
winter at Tavistock House; and, with the exception of his
rooms in Wellington Street, he had now no settled residence
but Gad's Hill Place. He sought its pleasant retreat about
the beginning of June, after the new experience of an attack
of rheumatism had made him recognise "the necessity of
country training all through the summer." Yet such was
the recuperative power, or the indomitable self-confidence,
of his nature, that after he had in these summer months
contributed some of the most delightful *Uncommercial
Traveller* papers to his journal, we find him already in
August "prowling about, meditating a new book."

It is refreshing to think of Dickens in this pleasant
interval of country life, before he had rushed once more
into the excitement of his labours as a public reader. We
may picture him to ourselves, accompanied by his dogs,
striding along the country roads and lanes, exploring the

M

haunts of the country tramps, " a piece of Kentish road,"
for instance, "bordered on either side by a wood, and having
on one hand, between the road dust and the trees, a skirt-
ing patch of grass. Wild flowers grow in abundance on
this spot, and it lies high and airy, with a distant river
stealing steadily away to the ocean like a man's life.
To gain the milestone here, which the moss, primroses,
violets, bluebells, and wild roses would soon render
illegible but for peering travellers pushing them aside
with their sticks, you must come up a steep hill come
which way you may." At the foot of that hill, I fancy,
lay Dullborough town half asleep in the summer afternoon; and the river in the distance was that which
bounded the horizon of a little boy's vision "whose
father's family name was Pirrip, and whose christian-
name was Philip, but whose infant tongue could make
of both names nothing longer or more explicit than Pip."

The story of Pip's adventures, the novel of *Great
Expectations*, was thought over in these Kentish per-
ambulations between Thames and Medway along the road
which runs, apparently with the intention of running
out to sea, from Higham towards the marshes; in the
lonely churchyard of Cooling village by the thirteen little
stone-lozenges, of which Pip counted only five, now nearly
buried in their turn by the rank grass; and in quiet
saunters through the familiar streets of Rochester, past
the "queer" town hall; and through the "Vines" past
the fine old Restoration House, called in the book (by
the name of an altogether different edifice) Satis House.
And the climax of the narrative was elaborated on a
unique steamboat excursion from London to the mouth of
the Thames, broken by a night at the Ship and Lobster,
an old riverside inn called The Ship in the story. No

wonder that Dickens' descriptive genius should become
refreshed by these studies of his subject, and that thus
Great Expectations should have indisputably become one
of the most picturesque of his books. But it is something very much more at the same time. The *Tale of Two
Cities* had as a story strongly seized upon the attention
of the reader. But in the earlier chapters of *Great
Expectations* everyone felt that Dickens was himself
again. Since the Yarmouth scenes in *David Copperfield* he had written nothing in which description married
itself to sentiment so humorously and so tenderly.
Uncouth, and slow, and straightforward, and gentle
of heart, like Mr. Peggotty, Joe Gargery is as new
a conception as he is a genuinely true one ; nor
is it easy to know under what aspect to relish him
most, whether disconsolate in his Sunday clothes, "like
some extraordinary bird, standing, as he did, speech-
less, with his tuft of feathers ruffled, and his mouth
open as if he wanted a worm," or at home by his
own fireside, winking at his little comrade, and, when
caught in the act by his wife, "drawing the back of his
hand across his nose with his usual conciliatory air on
such occasions." Nor since *David Copperfield* had Dickens
again shown such an insight as he showed here into
the world of a child's mind. "To be quite sure," he
wrote to Forster, "I had fallen into no unconscious repetitions, I read *David Copperfield* again the other day, and
was affected by it to a degree you would hardly believe."
His fears were unnecessary ; for with all its charm the
history of Pip lacks the personal element which insures
our sympathy to the earlier story and to its hero. In
delicacy, of feeling, however, as well as in humour of
description, nothing in Dickens surpasses the earlier chap-

ters of *Great Expectations*; and equally excellent is the
narrative of Pip's disloyalty of heart towards his early
friends, down to his departure from the forge, a picture
of pitiable selfishness almost Rousseau-like in its fidelity
to poor human nature, down to his comic humiliation,
when in the pride of his new position and his new clothes,
before "that unlimited miscreant, Trabb's boy." The
later and especially the concluding portions of this novel
contain much that is equal in power to its opening; but
it must be allowed that, before many chapters have
ended, a false tone finds its way into the story. The
whole history of Miss Havisham, and the crew of relations
round the unfortunate creature, is strained and unnatural,
and Estella's hardness is as repulsive as that of Edith
Dombey herself. Mr. Jaggers and his housekeeper, and
even Mr. Wemmick, have an element of artificiality,
in them, while about the Pocket family there is little,
if anything at all, that is real. The story, however,
seems to recover itself as the main thread in its deftly-
woven texture is brought forward again; when on a
dark gusty night, ominous of coming trouble, the
catastrophe of Pip's expectations announces itself in the
return from abroad of his unknown benefactor, the convict
whom he had as a child fed on the marshes. The remainder
of the narrative is successful in conveying to the reader
the sense of sickening anxiety which fills the hero; the
interest is skilfully sustained by the introduction of a
very strong situation—Pip's narrow escape out of the
clutches of "Old Orlick" in the limekiln on the marshes;
and the climax is reached in the admirably-executed narrative of the convict's attempt, with the aid of Pip, to escape
by the river. The actual winding-up of *Great Expectations*
is not altogether satisfactory; but on the whole the book

a public to which he was by this time about the best known man in England, had he been warned that weakness and weariness were not to be avoided even by a nature endowed with faculties so splendid and with an energy so conquering as his. He seemed to stand erect in the strength of his matured powers, equal as of old to any task which he set himself, and exulting, though with less buoyancy of spirit than of old, in the wreaths which continued to strew his path. Yet already the ranks of his contemporaries were growing thinner, while close to himself death was taking away members of the generation before, and of that after, his own. Among them was his mother—of whom his biography and his works have little to say or to suggest—and his second son. Happy events, too, had in the due course of things contracted the family circle at Gad's Hill. Of his intimates, he lost, in 1863, Augustus Egg; and in 1864, John Leech, to whose genius he had himself formerly rendered eloquent homage.

A still older associate, the great painter Stanfield, survived till 1867; "no one of your father's friends," Dickens then wrote to Stanfield's son, "can ever have loved him more dearly than I always did, or can have better known the worth of his noble character." Yet another friend, who however, so far as I can gather, had not, at any time, belonged to Dickens' most familiar circle, had died on Christmas Eve, 1863—Thackeray, whom it had for some time become customary to compare or contrast with him as his natural rival. Yet in point of fact, save for the tenderness which, as with all humourists of the highest order, was an important element in their writings, and save for the influences of time and country to which they were both subject, there are hardly two other among our great humorists who have less in common. Their unlikeness shows itself, among other things, in the use made by Thackeray of suggestions which it is difficult to believe he did not in the first instance owe to Dickens. Who would venture to call Captain Costigan a plagiarism from Mr. Snevellici, or to assert that Wenham and Wagg were copied from Pyke and Pluck, or that Major Pendennis—whose pardon one feels inclined to beg for the juxtaposition — was founded upon Major Bagstock, or the Old Campaigner in the *Newcomes* on the Old Soldier in *Copperfield?* But that suggestions were in these and perhaps in a few other instances derived from Dickens by Thackeray for some of his most masterly characters, it would, I think, be idle to deny. In any case, the style of these two great writers differed as profoundly as their way of looking at men and things. Yet neither of them lacked a thorough appreciation of the other's genius; and it is pleasant to remember that after paying in *Pendennis* a tribute to the purity of Dickens' books, Thackeray, in a public lecture referred to his supposed rival in a way which elicited from the latter the warmest of acknowledgments. It cannot be said that the memorial words, which after Thackeray's death Dickens was prevailed upon to contribute to the *Cornhill Magazine,* did more than justice to the great writer whom England had just lost; but it is well that the kindly and unstinting tribute of admiration should remain on record, to contradict any supposition that a disagreement which had some years previously disturbed the harmony of their intercourse, and of which the world had, according to its wont, made the most, had really estranged two generous minds from one another. The effort which on this occasion Dickens made, is in itself a proof of his kindly feeling towards Thackeray. Of Talfourd and Landor and Stanfield, he could write readily

that the last of the *All the Year Round* Christmas
Numbers, the continuous story of *No Thoroughfare*,
was written by Dickens and Mr. Wilkie Collins in 1867
with a direct eye to its subsequent adaptation to the stage,
for which it actually was fitted by Mr. Wilkie Collins in
the following year.   The place of its production, the
Adelphi, suited the broad effects and the rather conventional comic humour of the story and piece.   From
America, Dickens watched the preparation of the piece
with unflagging interest; and his innate and irrepressible genius for stage-management reveals itself in the
following passage from a letter written by him to an
American friend soon after his return to England: " *No
Thoroughfare* is very shortly coming out in Paris, where
it is now in active rehearsal.   It is still playing here,
but without Fechter, who has been very ill.   He and
Wilkie raised so many pieces of stage-effect here, that,
unless I am quite satisfied with the report, I shall go over
and try my stage-managerial hand at the Vaudeville
Theatre.   I particularly want the drugging and attempted
robbery in the bedroom-scene at the Swiss Inn to be done
to the sound of a waterfall rising and falling with the
wind.   Although in the very opening of that scene they
speak of the waterfall, and listen to it, nobody thought of
its mysterious music.   I could make it, with a good stage-
carpenter, in an hour."

Great Expectations had been finished in 1860, and
already in the latter part of 1861, the year which comprised
the main portion of his second series of readings, he had
been thinking of a new story.   He had even found a
title—the unlucky title which he afterwards adopted—
but in 1862 the tempting Australian invitation had been
a serious obstacle in his way.   " I can force myself to go

aboard a ship, and I can force myself to do at that reading-desk what I have done a hundred times; but whether, with all this unsettled fluctuating distress in my mind, I could force an original book out of it, is another question." Nor was it the "unsettled fluctuating distress" which made it a serious effort for him to attempt another longer fiction. Dickens shared with most writers the experience that both the inventive power and the elasticity of memory decline with advancing years. Already since the time when he was thinking of writing *Little Dorrit* it had become his habit to enter in a book kept for the purpose, memoranda for possible future use, hints for subjects of stories,[1] scenes, situations, and characters; thoughts and fancies of all kinds; titles for possible books. Of these, *Somebody's Luggage, Our Mutual Friend,* and *No Thoroughfare*—the last an old fancy revived—came to honourable use; as did many names, both christian and surnames, and combinations of both. Thus Bradley Headstone's *prænomen* was derived directly from the lists of the Education Department, and the Lammles and the Stiltstalkings, with Mr. Merdle and the Dorrits, existed as names before the characters were fitted to them. All this, though no doubt in part attributable to the playful readiness of an observation never to be caught asleep, points in the direction of a desire to be securely provided with an armoury of which, in earlier days, he would have taken slight thought.

Gradually, indeed, so far as I know, more gradually than in the case of any other of his stories, he had built up the tale for which he had determined on the title of

---

[1] Dickens undoubtedly had a genius for titles. Among some which he suggested for the use of a friend and contributor to his journal, are " *What will he do with it ?* " and " *Can he forgive her ?* "

Our Mutual Friend, and slowly, and without his old self-confidence, he had, in the latter part of 1863, set to work upon it. "I want to prepare it for the spring, but I am determined not to begin to publish with less than four numbers done. I see my opening perfectly, with the one main line on which the story is to turn, and if I don't strike while the iron (meaning myself) is hot, I shall drift off again, and have to go through all this uneasiness once more." For, unfortunately, he had resolved on returning to the old twenty-number measure for his new story. Begun with an effort, *Our Mutual Friend*—the publication of which extended from May, 1864, to November, 1865—was completed under difficulties, and difficulties of a kind hitherto unknown to Dickens. In February, 1865, as an immediate consequence, perhaps, of exposure at a time when depression of spirits rendered him less able than usual to bear it, he had a severe attack of illness, of which Forster says that it "put a broad mark between his past life and what remained to him of the future." From this time forward he felt a lameness in his left foot, which continued to trouble him at intervals during the remainder of his life, and which finally communicated itself to the left hand. A comparison of times, however, convinced Forster that the real origin of this ailment was to be sought in general causes.

In 1865, as the year wore on, and the pressure of the novel still continued, he felt that he was "working himself into a damaged state," and was near to that which has greater terrors for natures like his than for more placid temperaments—breaking down. So, in May, he went first to the seaside and then to France. On his return— it was the 9th of June, the date of his death five years

afterwards—he was in the railway train which met with a
fearful accident at Staplehurst, in Kent.   His carriage
was the only passenger-carriage in the train which, when
the bridge gave way, was not thrown over into the stream.
He was able to escape out of the window, to make his way
in again for his brandy-flask and the MS. of a number of
Our Mutual Friend which he had left behind him, to
clamber down the brickwork of the bridge for water,
to do what he could towards rescuing his unfortunate
fellow-travellers, and to aid the wounded and the
dying.   "I have," he wrote, in describing the scene,
" a—I don't know what to call it : constitutional, I
suppose—presence of mind, and was not in the least
fluttered at the time. . . . But in writing these scanty
words of recollection, I feel the shake and am obliged to
stop."   Nineteen months afterwards, when on a hurried
reading tour in the North, he complains to Miss Hogarth
of the effect of the railway shaking which since the Staplehurst accident "tells more and more."   It is clear how
serious a shock the accident had caused.   He never, Miss
Hogarth thinks, quite recovered it.   Yet it might have
acted less disastrously upon a system not already nervously
weakened.   As evidence of the decline of Dickens' nervous
power, I hardly know whether it is safe to refer to the
gradual change in his handwriting, which in his last years
is a melancholy study.

All these circumstances should be taken into account
in judging of Dickens' last completed novel.   The
author would not have been himself, had he, when once
fairly engaged upon his work, failed to feel something of
his old self-confidence.   Nor was this feeling, which he
frankly confessed to Mr. Wilkie Collins, altogether unwar-

ranted. *Our Mutual Friend*[1] is, like the rest of Dickens'
later writings, carefully and skilfully put together as a
story. No exception is to be taken to it on the ground
that the identity on which much of the plot hinges is
long foreseen by the reader ; for this, as Dickens told his
critics in his postscript, had been part of his design, and
was, in fact, considering the general nature of the story,
almost indispensable. The defect rather lies in the absence
of that element of uncertainty which is needed in order
to sustain the interest. The story is, no doubt, ingeniously
enough constructed, but admiration of an ingenious construction is insufficient to occupy the mind of a reader
through an inevitable disentanglement. Moreover, some
of the machinery, though cleverly contrived, cannot be said
to work easily. Thus, the *ruse* of the excellent Boffin in
playing the part of a skinflint might pass as a momentary
device, but its inherent improbability, together with the
likelihood of its leading to an untoward result, makes its
protraction undeniably tedious. It is not, however, in
my opinion at least, in the matter of construction that
Our Mutual Friend presents a painful contrast with earlier
works produced, like it, "on a large canvas." The conduct of the story as a whole is fully vigorous enough to
enchain the attention ; and in portions of it the hand of
the master displays its unique power. He is at his best
in the whole of the waterside scenes, both where The
Six Jolly Fellowship Porters (identified by zealous dis-

---

[1] This title has helped to extinguish the phrase of which it
consists. Few would now be found to agree with the last clause
of Flora's parenthesis in *Little Dorrit* : " Our mutual friend—too
cold a word for me ; at least I don't mean that, very proper
expression, mutual friend."

coverers with a tavern called The Two Brewers), lies like
an oasis in the midst of a desert of ill-favoured tidal
deposits, and where Rogue Riderhood has his lair at the
lock higher up the river. A marvellous union of observation and imagination was needed for the picturing of a world
in which this amphibious monster has his being; and
never did Dickens' inexhaustible knowledge of the physiognomy of the Thames and its banks stand him in better
stead than in these powerful episodes. It is unfortunate, though in accordance with the common fate of heroes
and heroines, that Lizzie Hexham should, from the outset,
have to discard the colouring of her surroundings, and
to talk the conventional dialect as well as express the conventional sentiments of the heroic world. Only at the
height of the action she ceases to be commonplace, and
becomes entitled to be remembered among the true
heroines of fiction. A more unusual figure, of the half-
pathetic, half-grotesque kind for which Dickens had a
peculiar liking, is Lizzie's friend, the dolls' dressmaker,
into whom he has certainly infused an element of genuine
sentiment; her protector, Riah, on the contrary, is a mere
stage-saint, though by this character Dickens appears to
have actually hoped to redeem the aspersions he was supposed to have cast upon the Jews, as if Riah could have
redeemed Fagin any more than Sheva redeemed Shylock.

But in this book whole episodes and parts of the plot
through which the mystery of John Harmon winds its
length along, are ill adapted for giving pleasure to any
reader. The whole Boffin, Wegg, and Venus business—if
the term may pass—is extremely wearisome; the character
of Mr. Venus, in particular, seems altogether unconnected
or unarticulated with the general plot, on which, indeed,
it is but an accidental excrescence. In the Wilfer family

there are the outlines of some figures of genuine humour,
but the outlines only; nor is Bella raised into the sphere of
the charming out of that of the pert and skittish. A more
ambitious attempt, and a more noteworthy failure, was
the endeavour to give to the main plot of this novel such
a satiric foil as the Circumlocution Office had furnished
to the chief action of *Little Dorrit*, in a caricature of
society at large, its surface varnish and its internal rotten-
ness. The Barnacles, and those who deemed it their duty
to rally round the Barnacles, had, we saw, felt themselves
hard hit; but what sphere or section of society could
feel itself specially caricatured in the Veneerings, or in
their associates — the odious Lady Tippins, the im-
possibly brutal Podsnap, Fascination Fledgeby, and
the Lammles, a couple which suggests nothing but
antimony and the Chamber of Horrors? Caricature
such as this, representing no society that has ever
in any part of the world pretended to be "good," corresponds to the wild rhetoric of the superfluous Betty
Higden episode against the "gospel according to Pod-
snappery;" but it is, in truth, satire from which both wit
and humour have gone out. An angry, often almost
spasmodic, mannerism has to supply their place. Among
the personages moving in "society" are two which, as
playing serious parts in the progress of the plot, the
author is necessarily obliged to seek to endow with the
flesh and blood of real human beings. Yet it is precisely
in these—the friends Eugene and Mortimer—that, in the
earlier part of the novel at all events, the constraint of
the author's style seems least relieved; the dialogues
between these two Templars have an unnaturalness about
them as intolerable as euphuism or the effeminacies of
the Augustan age. It is true that, when the story reaches

its tragic height, the character of Eugene is borne along
with it, and his affectations are forgotten. But in previous
parts of the book, where he poses as a wit, and is evidently
meant for a gentleman, he fails to make good his claims
to either character. Even the skilfully contrived contrast
between the rivals Eugene Wrayburn and the school-
master Bradley Headstone—through whom and through
whose pupil, Dickens, by the way, dealt another blow
against a system of mental training founded upon facts
alone—fails to bring out the conception of Eugene which
the author manifestly had in his mind. Lastly, the old way
of reconciling dissonances—a marriage which "society"
calls a *mésalliance*—has rarely furnished a lamer ending
than here ; and, had the unwritten laws of English
popular fiction permitted, a tragic close would have better
accorded with the sombre hue of the most powerful
portions of this curiously unequal romance.

The effort—for such it was—of *Our Mutual Friend* had
not been over for more than a few months, when Dickens
accepted a proposal for thirty nights' readings from the
Messrs. Chappell ; and by April, 1866, he was again hard
at work, flying across the country into Lancashire and
Scotland, and back to his temporary London residence
in Southwick Place, Hyde Park. In any man more
capable than Dickens of controlling the restlessness which
consumed him, the acceptance of this offer would have
been incomprehensible ; for his heart had been declared
out of order by his physician, and the patient had shown
himself in some degree awake to the significance of this
opinion. But the readings were begun and accomplished
notwithstanding, though not without warnings, on which
he insisted on putting his own interpretation. Sleeplessness aggravated fatigue, and stimulants were already neces-

revels of the saloon, seems to have done him good, or at
least to have made him, as usual, impatient to be at his
task.   Barely arrived, he is found reporting himself "so
well, that I am constantly chafing at not having begun to-
night, instead of this night week."   By December, however, he was at his reading-desk, first at Boston, where he
met with the warmest of welcomes, and then at New York,
where there was a run upon the tickets, which he described
with his usual excited delight.   The enthusiasm of his
reception by the American public must have been
heightened by the thought that it was now or never for
them to see him face to face, and, bygones being bygones,
to testify to him their admiration.   But there may have
been some foundation for his discovery that some signs
of agitation on his part were expected in return, and
"that it would have been taken as a suitable compliment
if I would stagger on the platform, and instantly drop,
overpowered by the spectacle before me."   It was but a
sad Christmas which he spent with his faithful Dolby
at their New York inn, tired, and with a "genuine
American catarrh upon him," of which he never freed
himself during his stay in the country.   Hardly had he
left the doctor's hands, than he was about again, reading
in Boston and New York and their more immediate neighbourhood—that is within six or seven hours by railway—
till February; and then, in order to stimulate his public,
beginning a series of appearances at more distant places
before returning to his starting-points.   His whole tour
included, besides a number of New England towns,
Philadelphia, Baltimore and Washington, and in the north
Cleveland and Buffalo.   Canada and the West were struck
out of the programme, the latter chiefly because exciting
political matters were beginning to absorb public attention.

During these journeyings Dickens gave himself up altogether to the business of his readings, only occasionally allowing himself to accept the hospitality proffered him on every side. Thus only could he breast the difficulties of his enterprise; for, as I have said, his health was never good during the whole of his visit, and his exertions were severe, though eased by the self-devotion of his attendants, of which, as of his constant kindness, both serious and sportive, towards them, it is touching to read. Already in January, he describes himself as not seldom "so dead beat" at the close of a reading "that they lay me down on a sofa, after I have been washed and dressed, and I lie there, extremely faint, for a quarter of an hour," and as suffering from intolerable sleeplessness at night. His appetite was equally disordered, and he lived mainly on stimulants. Why had he condemned himself to such a life?

When at last he could declare the stress of his work over, he described himself as "nearly used up. Climate, distance, catarrh, travelling, and hard work, have begun —I may say so, now they are nearly all over—to tell heavily upon me. Sleeplessness besets me; and if I had engaged to go on into May, I think I must have broken down." Indeed, but for his wonderful energy and the feeling of exultation which is derived from a heavy task nearly accomplished, he would have had to follow the advice of " Longfellow and all the Cambridge men," and give in nearly at the last. But he persevered through the farewell readings, both at Boston and at New York, though on the night before the last reading in America, he told Dolby that if he "had to read but twice more, instead of once, he couldn't do it." This last reading of all was given at New York on April 20th, two days after a farewell banquet at Delmonico's. It was

when speaking on this occasion that, very naturally
moved by the unalloyed welcome which had greeted
him in whatever part of the States he had visited,
he made the declaration already mentioned, promising to
perpetuate his grateful sense of his recent American
experiences.   This apology, which was no apology, at
least remains one among many proofs of the fact, that
with Dickens kindness never fell on a thankless soil.

The merry month of May was still young in the Kentish
fields and lanes when the master of Gad's Hill Place was
home again at last.   "I had not been at sea three days
on the passage home," he wrote to his friend Mrs. Watson,
"when I became myself again."   It was, however, too
much, when "a 'deputation'—two in number, of whom
only one could get into my cabin, while the other looked
in at my window—came to ask me to read to the passengers
that evening in the saloon.   I respectfully replied that
sooner than do it I would assault the captain and be put
in irons."   Alas! he was already fast bound, by an engagement concluded soon after he had arrived in Boston, to a
final series of readings at home.   "Farewell" is a difficult
word to say for anyone who has grown accustomed to the
stimulating excitement of a public stage, and it is not
wonderful that Dickens should have wished to see the
faces of his familiar friends—the English public—once
more.   But the engagement to which he had set his
hand was for a farewell of a hundred readings, at the
recompense of eight thousand pounds, in addition to ex-
penses and percentage.   It is true that he had done this
before he had fully realised the effect of his American
exertions; but even so, there was a terrible unwisdom in
the promise.   These last readings—and he alone is, in
common fairness, to be held responsible for the fact—cut

short a life from which much noble fruit might still have
been expected for our literature, and which in any case
might have been prolonged as a blessing beyond all that
gold can buy to those who loved him.

Meanwhile, he had allowed himself a short respite,
before resuming his labours in October. It was not more,
his friends thought, than he needed, for much of his old
buoyancy seemed to them to be wanting in him, except
when hospitality or the intercourse of friendship called it
forth. What a charm there still was in his genial humour
his letters would suffice to show. It does one good
to read his description to his kind American friends
Mr. and Mrs. Fields of his tranquillity at Gad's Hill :
"Divers birds sing here all day, and the nightingales
all night. The place is lovely, and in perfect order. I
have put five mirrors in the Swiss châlet where I write,
and they reflect and refract in all kinds of ways the
leaves that are quivering at the windows, and the great
fields of waving corn, and the sail-dotted river. My room
is up among the branches of the trees, and the birds and
the butterflies fly in and out, and the green branches shoot
in at the open windows, and the lights and shadows of the
clouds come and go with the rest of the company. The
scent of the flowers, and indeed of everything that is
growing for miles and miles, is most delicious."

Part of this rare leisure he generously devoted to the
preparation for the press of a volume of literary remains
from the pen of an old friend. The *Religious Opinions
of Chauncey Hare Townshend* should not be altogether
overlooked by those interested in Dickens, to whom the
loose undogmatic theology of his friend commended itself
as readily as the sincere religious feeling underlying it.
I cannot say what answer Dickens would have returned

to an inquiry as to his creed, but the nature of his religious opinions is obvious enough. Born in the Church of England, he had so strong an aversion from what seemed to him dogmatism of any kind, that he for a time—in 1843— connected himself with a Unitarian congregation ; and to Unitarian views his own probably continued during his life most nearly to approach. He described himself as "morally wide asunder from Rome," but the religious conceptions of her community cannot have been a matter of anxious inquiry with him, while he was too liberal-minded to be, unless occasionally, aggressive in his Protestantism. For the rest, his mind, though imaginative, was without mystical tendencies, while for the transitory superstitions of the day it was impossible but that he should entertain the contempt which they deserved ; "although," he writes—

> I regard with a hushed and solemn fear, the mysteries, between which, and this state of existence, is interposed the barrier of the great trial and change that fall on all the things that live; and, although I have not the audacity to pretend that I know anything of them, I cannot reconcile the mere banging of doors, ringing of bells, creaking of boards, and such like insignificances, with the majestic beauty and pervading analogy of all the Divine rules that I am permitted to understand.

His piety was undemonstrative and sincere, as his books alone would suffice to prove ; and he seems to have sought to impress upon his children those religious truths with the acceptance and practice of which he remained himself content. He loved the New Testament, and had, after some fashion of his own, paraphrased the Gospel narrative for the use of his children ; but he thought that "half the misery and hypocrisy of the Christian world arises from a stubborn determination to refuse the New Testament as a sufficient guide in itself, and to force the Old Testament into alliance with it—whereof comes all manner

of camel-swallowing and of gnat-straining." Of Puritanism
in its modern forms he was an uncompromising, and no
doubt a conscientious, opponent; and though, with perfect sincerity, he repelled the charge that his attacks upon
cant were attacks upon religion, yet their *animus* is such
as to make the misinterpretation intelligible.   His dissent-
ing ministers are of the *Bartholomew Fair* species, and
though, in his later books, a good clergyman here and
there makes his modest appearance, the balance can hardly
be said to be satisfactorily redressed.

The performance of this pious office was not the only
kind act he did after his return from America.   Of course,
however, his own family was nearest to his heart.   No
kinder or more judicious words were ever addressed by a
father to his children than those which, about this time,
he wrote to one of his sons, then beginning a successful
career at Cambridge, and to another—the youngest—who
was setting forth for Australia, to join an elder brother
already established in that country.   "Poor Plorn," he
afterwards wrote, "is gone to Australia.   It was a hard
parting at the last.   He seemed to me to become once
more my youngest and favourite child as the day drew
near, and I did not think I could have been so shaken."

In October his "farewell" readings began.   He had
never had his heart more in the work than now.   Curiously
enough, not less than two proposals had reached him
during this autumn—one from Birmingham and the other
from Edinburgh—that he should allow himself to be put
forward as a candidate for Parliament; but he declined to
entertain either, though in at least one of the two cases
the prospects of success would not have been small.   His
views of political and parliamentary life had not changed
since he had written to Bulwer Lytton in 1865: "Would

there not seem to be something horribly rotten in the system of political life, when one stands amazed how any man, not forced into it by his position, as you are, can bear to live it?" Indeed, they had hardly changed since the days when he had come into personal contact with them as a reporter. In public and in private he had never ceased to ridicule our English system of party, and to express his contempt for the Legislature and all its works. He had, however, continued to take a lively interest in public affairs, and his letters contain not a few shrewd remarks on both home and foreign questions. Like most liberal minds of his age, he felt a warm sympathy for the cause of Italy; and the English statesman whom he appears to have most warmly admired was Lord Russell, in whose good intentions neither friends nor adversaries were wont to lose faith. Meanwhile, his radicalism gradually became of the most thoroughly independent type, though it interfered neither with his approval of the proceedings in Jamaica as an example of strong government, nor with his scorn of "the meeting of jawbones and asses," held against Governor Eyre at Manchester. The political questions, however, which really moved him deeply were those social problems to which his sympathy for the poor had always directed his attention: the poor law, temperance, Sunday observance, punishment and prisons, labour and strikes. On all these heads sentiment guided his judgment, but he spared no pains to convince himself that he was in the right: and he was always generous, as when, notwithstanding his interest in *Household Words*, he declared himself unable to advocate the repeal of the paper duty for a moment, "as against the soap duty, or any other pressing on the mass of the poor."

Thus he found no difficulty in adhering to the course he

had marked out for himself. The subject which now occupied him before all others was a scheme for a new reading, with which it was his wish to vary and to intensify the success of the series on which he was engaged. This was no other than a selection of scenes from *Oliver Twist*, culminating in the scene of the murder of Nancy by Sikes, which, before producing it in public, he resolved to "try" upon a select private audience. The trial was a brilliant success; "the public," exclaimed a famous actress who was present, "have been looking out for a sensation these last fifty years or so, and, by heaven, they have got it!" Accordingly, from January, 1869, it formed one of the most frequent of his readings, and the effort which it involved counted for much in the collapse which was to follow. Never were the limits between reading and acting more thoroughly effaced by Dickens, and never was the production of an extraordinary effect more equally shared by author and actor. But few who witnessed this extraordinary performance can have guessed the elaborate preparation bestowed upon it, which is evident from the following notes (by Mr. C. Kent) on the book used in it by the reader:

What is as striking as anything in all this reading, however—that is, in the reading copy of it now lying before us as we write—is the mass of hints as to the byplay in the stage directions for himself, so to speak, scattered up and down the margin. "Fagin raised his right hand, and shook his trembling forefinger in the air," is there on page 101 in print. Beside it, on the margin in MS., is the word "*Action.*" Not a word of it was said. It was simply *done.* Again, immediately below that, on the same page —Sikes *loquitur* : "Oh! you haven't, haven't you?" passing a pistol into a more convenient pocket ("*Action*" again in MS. on the margin). Not a word was said about the pistol. . . . So again, afterwards, as a rousing self-direction, one sees notified in MS. on page 107, the grim stage direction, "*Murder coming!*"

The "Murder" was frequently read by Dickens not less than four times a week during the early months of 1869, in which year, after beginning in Ireland, he had been continually travelling to and fro between various parts of Great Britain and town. Already in February the old trouble in his foot had made itself felt, but, as usual, it had long been disregarded. On the 10th of April he had been entertained at Liverpool, in St. George's Hall, at a banquet presided over by Lord Dufferin, and in a genial speech had tossed back the ball to Lord Houghton, who had pleasantly bantered him for his unconsciousness of the merits of the House of Lords. Ten days afterwards, he was to read at Preston, but, feeling uneasy about himself, had reported his symptoms to his doctor in London. The latter hastened down to Preston, and persuaded Dickens to accompany him back to town, where, after a consultation, it was determined that the readings must be stopped for the current year, and that reading combined with travelling must never be resumed. What his sister-in-law and daughter feel themselves justified in calling "the beginning of the end" had come at last.

With his usual presence of mind, Dickens at once perceived the imperative necessity of interposing "as it were, a fly-leaf in the book of my life, in which nothing should be written from without for a brief season of a few weeks." But he insisted that the combination of the reading and the travelling was alone to be held account-able for his having found himself feeling, "for the first time in my life, giddy, jarred, shaken, faint, uncertain of voice and sight and tread and touch, and dull of spirit." Meanwhile he for once kept quiet, first in London, and then at Gad's Hill. "This last summer," say those who did most to make it bright for him, " was a very happy one," and gladdened by the visits of many friends. On the retirement, also on account of ill-health, from *All the Year Round*, of his second self, Mr. W. H. Wills, he was fortunately able at once to supply the vacant place by the appointment to it of his eldest son, who seems to have inherited that sense of lucid order which was among his father's most distinctive characteristics. He travelled very little this year, though in September he made a speech at Birmingham on behalf of his favourite Midland Institute, delivering himself, at its conclusion, of an antithetical radical commonplace, which, being misreported or misunderstood, was commented upon with much unnecessary wonderment. With a view to avoiding the danger of excessive fatigue, the latter part of the year was chiefly devoted to writing in advance part of his new book, which, like *Great Expectations*, was to grow up, and to be better for growing up, in his own Kentish home, and almost within sound of the bells of "Cloisterham" Cathedral. But the new book was never to be finished.

The first number of *The Mystery of Edwin Drood* was not published till one more short series of twelve readings, given in London during a period extending from January to March, was at an end. He had obtained Sir Thomas Watson's consent to his carrying out this wish, largely caused by the desire to compensate the Messrs. Chappell in some measure for the disappointment to which he had been obliged to subject them by the interruption of his longer engagement. Thus, though the Christmas of 1869 had brought with it another warning of trouble in the foot, the year 1870 opened busily, and early in January Dickens established himself for the season at 5, Hyde

Park Place. Early in the month he made another speech
at Birmingham ; but the readings were strictly confined
to London. On the other hand, it was not to be
expected that the "Murder" would be excluded from the
list. It was read in January, to an audience of actors
and actresses; and it is pleasant to think that he was
able to testify to his kindly feeling towards their profession on one of the last occasions when he appeared on his
own stage. "I set myself," he wrote, "to carrying out of
themselves and their observation, those who were bent on
watching how the effects were got ; and, I believe, I succeeded. Coming back to it again, however, I feel it was
madness ever to do it so continuously. My ordinary
pulse is seventy-two, and it runs up under this effort
to one hundred and twelve." Yet this fatal reading was
repeated thrice more before the series closed, and with
even more startling results upon the reader. The
careful observations made by his physician, however,
show that the excitement of the last readings was altogether too great for any man to have endured much
longer. At last, on March 16th, the night came
which closed fifteen years of personal relations between
the English public and its favourite author, such as are,
after all, unparalleled in the history of our literature.
His farewell words were few and simple ; and referred
with dignity to his resolution to devote himself henceforth exclusively to his calling as an author, and to his
hope that in but two short weeks' time his audience
"might enter, in their own homes, on a new series of
readings at which his assistance would be indispensable."

Of the short time which remained to him his last book
was the chief occupation ; and an association thus clings
to the *Mystery of Edwin Drood*, which would, in any

case, incline us to treat this fragment—for it was to be no
more—with tenderness. One would, indeed, hardly be justified in asserting that this story, like that which Thackeray
left behind him in the same unfinished state, bade fair to
become a masterpiece in its author's later manner; there is
much that is forced in its humour, while as to the working
out of the chief characters our means of judgment are of
course incomplete. The outline of the design, on the other
hand, presents itself with tolerable clearness to the minds
of most readers of insight or experience, though the story
deserves its name of a mystery, instead of, like *Our
Mutual Friend*, seeming merely to withhold a necessary
explanation. And it must be allowed that few plots have
ever been more effectively laid than this, of which the
untying will never be known. Three such personages in
relation to a deed of darkness as Jasper for its contriver,
Durden for its unconscious accomplice, and Deputy for its
self-invited witness, and all so naturally connecting themselves with the locality of the perpetration of the crime,
assuredly could not have been brought together, except
by one who had gradually attained to mastership in the
adaptation of characters to the purposes of a plot. Still,
the strongest impression left upon the reader of this fragment, is the evidence it furnishes of Dickens having
retained to the last powers which were most peculiarly
and distinctively his own. Having skilfully brought into
connexion, for the purposes of his plot, two such
strangely-contrasted spheres of life and death, as the
cathedral close at "Cloisterham" and an opium-smoking
den in one of the obscurest corners of London, he is
enabled, by his imaginative and observing powers, not
only to *realise* the picturesque elements in both scenes,
but also to convert them into a twofold background, accom-

modating itself to the most vivid hues of human passion.
This is to bring out what he was wont to call "the romantic
aspect of familiar things." With the physiognomy of
Cloisterham—otherwise Rochester—with its cathedral,
and its "monastery" ruin, and its "Minor Canon Corner,"
and its "Nuns' House"—otherwise "Eastgate House," in
the High Street—he was, of course, closely acquainted ;
but he had never reproduced its features with so artistic a
cunning, and the Mystery of Edwin Drood will always
haunt Bishop Gundulph's venerable building and its
tranquil precincts. As for the opium-smoking, we have
his own statement, that what he described he saw—"exactly
as he had described it, penny ink-bottle and all—down in
Shadwell" in the autumn of 1869. "A couple of the
Inspectors of Lodging-houses knew the woman, and took
me to her as I was making a round with them, to see for
myself the working of Lord Shaftesbury's Bill." Between
these scenes, John Jasper—a figure conceived with singular
force—moves to and fro, preparing his mysterious design.
No story of the kind ever began more finely ; and we may
be excused from inquiring whether signs of diminished
vigour of invention and freshness of execution are to be
found in other and less prominent portions of the great
novelist's last work.

Before, in this year 1870, Dickens withdrew from London
to Gad's Hill, with the hope of there in quiet carrying his all
but half-finished task to its close, his health had not been
satisfactory ; he had suffered from time to time in his foot,
and his weary and aged look was observed by many of his
friends. He was able to go occasionally into society ;
though at the last dinner-party which he attended—
it was at Lord Houghton's, to meet the Prince of Wales
and the King of the Belgians—he had been unable to

mount above the dining-room floor. Already in March the Queen had found a suitable opportunity for inviting him to wait upon her at Buckingham Palace, when she had much gratified him by her kindly manner; and a few days later he made his appearance at the levee. These acknowledgments of his position as an English author were as they should be; no others were offered, nor is it a matter of regret that there should have been no titles to inscribe on his tomb. He was also twice seen on one of those public occasions which no eloquence graced so readily and so pleasantly as his: once in April, at the dinner for the Newsvendors' Charity, when he spoke of the existence among his humble clients of that "feeling of brotherhood and sympathy which is worth much to all men, or they would herd with wolves;" and once in May—only a day or two before he went home into the country—when at the Royal Academy dinner, he paid a touching tribute to the eminent painter, Daniel Maclise, who in the good old days had been much like a brother to himself. Another friend and companion, Mark Lemon, passed away a day or two afterwards; and with the most intimate of all, his future biographer, he lamented the familiar faces of their companions—not one of whom had passed his sixtieth year —upon which they were not to look again. On the 30th of May he was once more at Gad's Hill.

Here he forthwith set to work on his book, taking walks as usual, though of no very great length. On Thursday, the 9th of June, he had intended to pay his usual weekly visit to the office of his journal, and accordingly, on the 8th, devoted the afternoon as well as the morning to finishing the sixth number of the story. When he came across to the house from the châlet before dinner, he seemed, to his sister-in-law, who alone of the family was at home,

tired and silent, and, no sooner had they sat down to
dinner, than she noticed how seriously ill he looked. It
speedily became evident that a fit was upon him. "Come
and lie down," she entreated. "Yes, on the ground," he
said, very distinctly—these were the last words he spoke
—and he slid from her arm, and fell upon the floor. He
was laid on a couch in the room, and there he remained
unconscious almost to the last. He died at ten minutes
past six on the evening of the 9th—by which time his
daughters and his eldest son had been able to join the
faithful watcher by his side ; his sister and his son Henry
arrived when all was over.

His own desire had been to be buried near Gad's Hill ;
though at one time he is said to have expressed a wish
to lie in a disused graveyard, which is still pointed out, in
a secluded corner in the moat of Rochester Castle. Preparations had been made accordingly, when the Dean and
Chapter of Rochester urged a request that his remains might
be placed in their Cathedral. This was assented to ; but at
the last moment the Dean of Westminster gave expression to
a widespread wish that the great national writer might lie
in the national Abbey. There he was buried on June
14th, without the slightest attempt at the pomp which he
had deprecated in his will, and which he almost fiercely
condemned in more than one of his writings. "The funeral,"
writes Dean Stanley, whose own dust now mingles with that
of so many illustrious dead, "was strictly private. It took
place at an early hour in the summer morning, the grave
having been dug in secret the night before, and the vast
solitary space of the Abbey was occupied only by the
small band of the mourners, and the Abbey clergy, who,
without any music except the occasional peal of the organ,
read the funeral service. For days the spot was visited

by thousands; many were the tears shed by the poorer visitors. He rests beside Sheridan, Garrick, and Henderson"—the first actor ever buried in the Abbey. Associations of another kind cluster near; but his generous spirit would not have disdained the thought that he would seem even in death the players' friend.

A plain memorial brass on the walls of Rochester Cathedral vindicates the share which the ancient city and its neighbourhood will always have in his fame. But most touching of all it is to think of him under the trees of his own garden on the hill, in the pleasant home where, after so many labours and so many wanderings, he died in peace, and as one who had earned his rest.

CHAPTER VII.

THE FUTURE OF DICKENS' FAME.

THERE is no reason whatever to believe that in the few years which have gone by since Dickens' death the delight taken in his works throughout England and North America, as well as elsewhere, has diminished, or that he is not still one of our few most popular writers. The mere fact that his popularity has remained such since, nearly half a century ago he, like a beam of spring sunshine, first made the world gay, is a sufficient indication of the influence which he must have exercised upon his age. In our world of letters his followers have been many, though naturally enough those whose original genius impelled them to follow their own course soonest ceased to be his imitators. Among these I know no more signal instance than the great novelist whose surpassing merits he had very swiftly recognised in her earliest work. For though in the *Scenes of Clerical Life* George Eliot seems to be, as it were, hesitating between Dickens and Thackeray as the models of her humorous writing, reminiscences of the former are unmistakeable in the opening of *Amos Barton*, in *Mr. Gilfil's Love-Story*, in *Janet's Repentance*; and though it would be hazardous to trace his influence in the domestic scenes in *Adam Bede*, neither a Christmas exordium in one of the books of *The Mill on the Floss*, nor the Sam Weller-like freshness of Bob Jakin in the same powerful story, is altogether the author's own. Two of the most successful continental novelists of the present day have gone to school with Dickens: the one the truly national writer whose *Debit and Credit*, a work largely in the manner of his English model, has, as a picture of modern life, remained unexcelled in German literature ;[1] the other, the brilliant Southerner, who may write as much of the *History of his Books* as his public may desire to learn, but who cannot write the pathos of Dickens altogether out of *Jack*, or his farcical fun out of *Le Nabab*. And again—for I am merely illustrating, not attempting to describe, the literary influence of Dickens —who could fail to trace in the Californian studies and sketches of Bret Harte elements of humour and of pathos, to which that genuinely original author would be the last to deny that his great English "Master" was no stranger ?

Yet popularity and literary influence, however wide and however strong, often pass away as they have come ; and in no field of literature are there many reputations which the sea of time fails before very long to submerge. In prose fiction—a comparatively young literary growth—they are certainly not the most numerous, perhaps because on works of this species the manners and style of an age most readily impress themselves, rendering them proportionately strange to the ages that come after. In the works of even the lesser playwrights who pleased the liberal times of Elizabeth, and in lyrics of even secondary merit that were admired

---

[1] In the last volume of his *magnum opus* of historical fiction, Gustav Freytag, describes "Boz" as about the year 1846, filling with boundless enthusiasm the hearts of young men and maidens in a small Silesian country town.

by fantastic Caroline cavaliers, we can still take pleasure.
But who can read many of the "standard" novels published as lately even as the days of George the Fourth?
The speculation is, therefore, not altogether idle, whether
Dickens saw truly when labouring, as most great men
do labour, in the belief that his work was not only
for a day.   Literary eminence was the only eminence he
desired, while it was one of the very healthiest elements
in his character, that whatever he was, he was thoroughly.
He would not have told anyone, as Fielding's author told
Mr. Booth at the sponging-house, that romance-writing " is
certainly the easiest work in the world ; " nor being what
he was, could he ever have found it such in his own case.
" Whoever," he declared, " is devoted to an art must be content to give himself wholly up to it, and to find his recompense in it."   And not only did he obey his own labour-
laws, but in the details of his work as a man of letters he
spared no pains and no exercise of self-control.   ' I am,"
he generously told a beginner, to whom he was counselling
patient endeavour, "an impatient and impulsive person
myself, but it has been for many years the constant effort
of my life to practise at my desk what I preach to you."
Never, therefore has a man of letters had a better claim
to be judged by his works.   As he expressly said in his
will, he wished for no other monument than his writings ;
and with their aid we, who already belong to a new
generation, and whose children will care nothing for the
gossip and the scandal of which he, like most popular
celebrities, was in his lifetime privileged or doomed to
become the theme, may seek to form some definite conception of his future place among illustrious Englishmen.

It would, of course, be against all experience to suppose
that to future generations Dickens, as a writer, will be all

that he was to his own. Much that constitutes the subject,
or at least furnishes the background, of his pictures of
English life, like the Fleet Prison and the Marshalsea,
has vanished, or is being improved off the face of the
land. The form, again, of Dickens' principal works may
become obsolete, as it was in a sense accidental. He was
the most popular novelist of his day; but should prose
fiction, or even the full and florid species of it which has
enjoyed so long-lived a favour ever be out of season, the
popularity of Dickens' books must experience an inevitable diminution. And even before that day arrives,
not all the works in a particular species of literature that
may to a particular age have seemed destined to live, will
have been preserved. Nothing is more surely tested by
time than that originality which is the secret of a writer's
continuing to be famous, and continuing to be read.

Dickens was not—and to whom in these latter ages of
literature could such a term be applied?—a self-made
writer. in the sense that he owed nothing to those who
had gone before him. He was most assuredly no classical
scholar,—how could he have been? But I should hesitate
to call him an ill-read man, though he certainly was neither
a great nor a catholic reader, and though he could not help
thinking about *Nicholas Nickleby* while he was reading the
Curse of Kehama. In his own branch of literature his judgment was sound and sure-footed. It was of course a happy
accident, that as a boy he imbibed that taste for good
fiction which is a thing inconceivable to the illiterate.
Sneers have been directed against the poverty of his book-
shelves in his earlier days of authorship; but I fancy
there were not many popular novelists in 1839 who would
have taken down with them into the country for a summer
sojourn, as Dickens did to Petersham, not only a couple

"*Humphry Clinker*," he writes, "is certainly Smollett's best. I am rather divided between *Peregrine Pickle* and *Roderick Random*, both extraordinarily good in their way, which is a way without tenderness ; but you will have to read them both, and I send the first volume of *Peregrine* as the richer of the two." An odd volume of *Peregrine* was one of the books with which the waiter at the *Holly Tree Inn* endeavoured to beguile the lonely Christmas of the snowed-up traveller, but the latter "knew every word of it already." In the *Lazy Tour*, "Thomas, now just able to grope his way along, in a doubled-up condition, was no bad embodiment of Commodore Trunnion." I have noted, moreover, coincidences of detail which bear witness to Dickens' familiarity with Smollett's works. To Lieutenant Bowling and Commodore Trunnion, as to Captain Cuttle, every man was a "brother," and to the Commodore, as to Mr. Smallweed, the most abusive substantive addressed to a woman admitted of intensification by the epithet "brimstone." I think Dickens had not forgotten the opening of the *Adventures of an Atom* when he wrote a passage in the opening of his own *Christmas Carol* ; and that the characters of Tom Pinch and Tommy Traddles—the former more especially—were not conceived without some thought of honest Strap. Furthermore, it was Smollett's example that probably suggested to Dickens the attractive jingle in the title of his *Nicholas Nickleby*. But these are for the most part mere details. The manner of Dickens as a whole resembles Fielding's more strikingly than Smollett's, as it was only natural that it should. The irony of Smollett is drier than was reconcileable with Dickens' nature ; it is only in the occasional extravagances of his humour that the former anticipates anything in the latter, and it is only the coarsest scenes of Dickens

Among the writers of Dickens' own age there were only two, or perhaps three, who in very different degrees and ways, exercised a noticeable influence upon his writings. He once declared to Washington Irving that he kept everything written by that delightful author upon "his shelves, and in his thoughts, and in his heart of hearts." And, doubtless, in Dickens' early days as an author the influence of the American classic may have aided to stimulate the imaginative element in his English admirer's genius, and to preserve him from a grossness of humour into which, after the *Sketches by Boz*, he very rarely allowed himself to lapse.   The two other writers were Carlyle, and, as I have frequently noted in previous chapters, the friend and fellow-labourer of Dickens' later manhood, Mr. Wilkie Collins.   It is no unique experience that the disciple should influence the master; and in this instance, perhaps with the co-operation of the examples of the modern French theatre, which the two friends had studied in common, Mr. Wilkie Collins' manner had, I think, no small share in bringing about a transformation in that of Dickens.   His stories thus gradually lost all traces of the older masters both in general method and in detail; while he came to condense and concentrate his effects in successions of skilfully-arranged scenes.   Dickens' debt to Carlyle was, of course, of another nature; and in his works the proofs are not few of his readiness to accept the teachings of one whom he declared he would "go at all times farther to see than any man alive."   There was something singular in the admiration these two men felt for one another; for Carlyle, after an acquaintance of almost thirty years, spoke of Dickens as "a most cordial, sincere, clear-sighted, quietly decisive, just, and loving man;" and there is not one of these epithets but seems well conof which humour, in the more limited sense of the word, and pathos are the twin products. And in Dickens both these were paramount powers, almost equally various in their forms and effective in their operation. According to M. Taine, Dickens, while he excels in irony of a particular sort, being an Englishman, is incapable of being gay. Such profundities are unfathomable to the readers of *Pickwick*; though the French critic may have generalised from Dickens' later writings only. His pathos is not less true than various, for the gradations are marked between the stern tragic pathos of *Hard Times*, the melting pathos of the *Old Curiosity Shop, Dombey and Son,* and *David Copperfield*, and the pathos of helplessness which appeals to us in Smike and Jo. But this sensibility would not have given us Dickens' gallery of living pictures, had it not been for the powers of imagination and observation which enabled him spontaneously to exercise it in countless directions. To the way in which his imagination enabled him to identify himself with the figments of his own brain he frequently testified; Dante was not more certain in his celestial and infernal topography than was Dickens as to " every stair in the little midshipman's house," and as to " every young gentleman's bedstead in Dr. Blimber's establishment." One particular class of phenomena may be instanced instead of many, in the observation and poetic reproduction of which his singular natural endowment continually manifested itself —I mean those of the weather. It is not, indeed, often that he rises to a fine image like that in the description of the night in which Ralph Nickleby, ruined and crushed, slinks home to his death.

The night was dark, and a cold wind blew, driving the clouds furiously and fast before it. There was one black gloomy mass that seemed to follow him: not hurrying in the wild chase with

the others, but lingering sullenly behind, and gliding darkly and
stealthily on.   He often looked back at this, and, more than
once, stopped to let it pass over; but, somehow, when he went
forward again, it was still behind him, coming mournfully and
slowly up, like a shadowy funeral train.

But he again and again enables us to feel, as if
the Christmas morning on which Mr. Pickwick ran
gaily down the slide, or as if the "very quiet" moon-
lit night in the midst of which a sudden sound, like the
firing of a gun or a pistol, startled the repose of Lincoln's
Inn Fields, were not only what we have often precisely
experienced in country villages or in London squares,
but as if they were the very morning and the very night
which we *must* experience, if we were feeling the glow of
wintry merriment, or the awful chill of the presentiment of
evil in a dead hour. In its lower form this combination of the
powers of imagination and observation has the rapidity of
wit, and, indeed, sometimes *is* wit.   The gift of suddenly
finding out what a man, a thing, a combination of man
and thing, is like—this, too, comes by nature ; and
there is something electrifying in its sudden exercise,
even on the most trivial occasions, as when Flora,
delighted with Little Dorrit's sudden rise to fortune,
requests to know all

about the good, dear, quiet little thing, and all the changes of
her fortunes, carriage people now, no doubt, and horses without
number most romantic, a coat-of-arms of course, and wild beasts
on their hind legs, showing it as if it was a copy they had done
with mouths from ear to ear, good gracious!

But nature, when she gifted Dickens with sensibility,
observation, and imagination, had bestowed upon him yet
another boon in the quality which seems more prominent

than any other in his whole being. The vigour of Dickens—a mental and moral vigour supported by a splendid physical organism—was the parent of some of his foibles; among the rest, of his tendency to exaggeration. No fault has been more frequently found with his workmanship than this; nor can he be said to have defended himself very successfully on this head when he declared that he did "not recollect ever to have heard or seen the charge of exaggeration made against a feeble performance, though, in its feebleness, it may have been most untrue." But without this vigour he could not have been creative as he was; and in him there were accordingly united with rare completeness a swift responsiveness to the impulses of humour and pathos, an inexhaustible fertility in discovering and inventing materials for their exercise, and the constant creative desire to give to these newly-created materials a vivid plastic form.

And the mention of this last-named gift in Dickens suggests the query whether, finally, there is anything in his *manner* as a writer which may prevent the continuance of his extraordinary popularity. No writer can be great without a manner of his own; and that Dickens had such a manner his most supercilious censurer will readily allow. His terse narrative power, often intensely humorous in its unblushing and unwinking gravity, and often deeply pathetic in its simplicity, is as characteristic of his manner as is the supreme felicity of phrase in which he has no equal. As to the latter, I should hardly know where to begin and where to leave off were I to attempt to illustrate it. But, to take two instances of different kinds of wit, I may cite a passage in Guster's narrative of her interview with Lady Dedlock: "And so I took the letter from her, and she said she had nothing to give me; and *I said I was poor myself,*

and consequently wanted nothing;" and, of a different kind,
the account in one of his letters of a conversation with
Macready, in which the great tragedian, after a solemn
but impassioned commendation of his friend's reading,
"put his hand upon my breast and pulled out his pocket-
handkerchief, and *I felt as if I were doing somebody to his
Werner.*" These, I think, were among the most characteristic merits of his style. It also, and more especially in
his later years, had its characteristic faults. The danger
of degenerating into mannerism is incident to every
original manner. There is mannerism in most of the
great English prose-writers of Dickens' age—in Carlyle,
in Macaulay, in Thackeray—but in none of them is there
more mannerism than in Dickens himself. In his earlier
writings, in *Nicholas Nickleby*, for instance (I do not, of
course, refer to the Portsmouth boards), and even in *Martin
Chuzzlewit*, there is much stageyness; but in his later works
his own mannerism had swallowed up that of the stage,
and, more especially in serious passages, his style had
become what M. Taine happily characterises as *le style
tourmenté.* His choice of words remained throughout
excellent, and his construction of sentences clear. He told
Mr. Wilkie Collins that "underlining was not his nature;"
and in truth he had no need to emphasise his expressions,
or to bid the reader "go back upon their meaning." He
recognised his responsibility, as a popular writer, in keeping
the vocabulary of the language pure; and in *Little Dorrit*
he even solemnly declines to use the French word *trousseau.*
In his orthography, on the other hand, he was not free
from Americanisms; and his interpunctuation was consistently odd. But these are trifles; his more important
mannerisms were, like many really dangerous faults of style,
only the excess of characteristic excellences. Thus it was

he who elaborated with unprecedented effect, that humorous species of paraphrase which, as one of the most imitable devices of his style, has also been the most persistently imitated.   We are all tickled when Grip, the raven, "issues orders for the instant preparation of innumerable kettles for purposes of tea ;" or when Mr. Pecksniff's eye is "piously upraised, with something of that expression which the poetry of ages has attributed to a domestic bird, when breathing its last amid the ravages of an electric storm ;" but in the end the device becomes a mere trick of circumlocution.   Another mannerism which grew upon Dickens, and was faithfully imitated by several of his disciples, was primarily due to his habit of turning a fact, fancy, or situation round on every side.   This consisted in the reiteration of a construction, or of part of a construction, in the strained rhetorical fashion to which he at last accustomed us in spite of ourselves, but to which we were loath to submit in his imitators.   These and certain other peculiarities, which it would be difficult to indicate without incurring the charge of hypercriticism, hardened as the style of Dickens hardened ; and, for instance, in the *Tale of Two Cities* his mannerisms may be seen side by side in glittering array.   By way of compensation, the occasional solecisms and vulgarisms of his earlier style (he only very gradually ridded himself of the cockney habit of punning) no longer marred his pages ; and he ceased to break or lapse occasionally, in highly-impassioned passages, into blank verse.

From first to last Dickens' mannerism, like everything which he made part of himself, was not merely assumed on occasion, but was, so to speak, absorbed into his nature. It shows itself in almost everything that he wrote in his later years, from the most carefully-elaborated chapters of his books down to the most deeply-felt passages of his most familiar correspondence, in the midst of the most genuine pathos and most exuberant humour of his books, and in the midst of the sound sense and unaffected piety of his private letters. Future generations may, for this very reason, be perplexed and irritated by what we merely stumbled at, and may wish that what is an element hardly separable from many of Dickens' compositions were away from them, as one wishes away from his signature that horrible flourish which in his letters he sometimes represents himself as too tired to append.

But no distaste for his mannerisms is likely to obscure the sense of his achievements in the branch of literature to which he devoted the full powers of his genius and the best energies of his nature. He introduced indeed no new species of prose fiction into our literature. In the historical novel he made two far from unsuccessful essays, in the earlier of which in particular—*Barnaby Rudge*—he showed a laudable desire to enter into the spirit of a past age; but he was without the reading or the patience of either the author of *Waverley* or the author of *The Virginians*, and without the fine historic enthusiasm which animates the broader workmanship of *Westward Ho*. For the purely imaginative romance, on the other hand, of which in some of his works Lord Lytton was the most prominent representative in contemporary English literature, Dickens' genius was not without certain affinities; but to feel his full strength, he needed to touch the earth with his feet. Thus it is no mere phrase to say of him that he found the ideal in the real, and drew his inspirations from the world around him. Perhaps the strongest temptation which ever seemed likely to divert him from the sounder forms in which his masterpieces were cast, lay in the

direction of the *novel with a purpose*, the fiction intended primarily and above all things to promote the
correction of some social abuse, or the achievement of
some social reform. But in spite of himself, to whom
the often voiceless cause of the suffering and the op-
pressed was at all times dearer than any mere literary
success, he was preserved from binding his muse, as his
friend Cruikshank bound his art, handmaid in a service
with which freedom was irreconcileable. His artistic
instinct helped him in this, and perhaps also the consciousness that where, as in *The Chimes* or in *Hard Times*,
he had gone furthest in this direction, there had been
something jarring in the result. Thus, under the influences
described above, he carried on the English novel mainly
in the directions which it had taken under its early
masters, and more especially in those in which the essential
attributes of his own genius prompted him to excel.

Among the elements on which the effect alike of the
novelist's and of the dramatist's work must, apart from
style and diction, essentially depend, that of construction
is obviously one of the most significant. In this Dickens
was, in the earlier period of his authorship, very far from
strong. This was due in part to the accident that he began
his literary career as a writer of *Sketches*, and that his first
continuous book, *Pickwick*, was originally designed as little
more than a string of such. It was due in a still greater
measure to the influence of those masters of English fiction
with whom he had been familiar from boyhood, above
all to Smollett. And though, by dint of his usual energy,
he came to be able to invent a plot so generally effective
as that of *A Tale of Two Cities*, or, I was about to say, of
The Mystery of Edwin Drood, yet on this head he had had
to contend against a special difficulty; I mean, of course,

P

the publication of most of his books in monthly or even weekly numbers. In the case of a writer both pathetic and humorous, the serial method of publication leads the public to expect its due allowance of both pathos and humour every month or week, even if each number, to borrow a homely simile applied in *Oliver Twist* to books in general, need not contain " the tragic and the comic scenes in as regular alternation as the layers of red and white in a side of streaky bacon." And again, as in a melodrama of the old school, each serial division has, if possible, to close emphatically, effectively, with a promise of yet stranger, more touching, more laughable things to come. On the other hand, with this form of publication repetition is frequently necessary by way of " reminder " to indolent readers, whose memory needs refreshing after the long pauses between the acts. Fortunately, Dickens abhorred living, as it were, from hand to mouth, and thus diminished the dangers to which, I cannot help thinking, Thackeray at times almost succumbed. Yet, notwithstanding, in the arrangement of his incidents and the contrivance of his plots it is often impossible to avoid noting the imperfection of the machinery, or at least the traces of effort. I have already said under what influences, in my opinion, Dickens acquired a constructive skill which would have been conspicuous in most other novelists.

If in the combination of parts the workmanship of Dickens was not invariably of the best, on the other hand in the invention of those parts themselves he excelled, his imaginative power and dramatic instinct combining to produce an endless succession of effective scenes and situations, ranging through almost every variety of the pathetic and the humorous. In no direction was nature a more powerful aid to art with him than in this.

From his very boyhood he appears to have possessed in a developed form what many others may possess in its germ, the faculty of converting into a scene—putting, as it were, into a frame—personages that came under his notice, and the background on which he saw them. Who can forget the scene in *David Copperfield*, in which the friendless little boy attracts the wonderment of the good people of the publichouse where—it being a special occasion—he has demanded a glass of their "very best ale, with a head to it"? In the autobiographical fragment already cited, where the story appears in almost the same words, Dickens exclaims:

> Here we stand, all three, before me now, in my study in Devonshire Terrace. The landlord, in his shirt-sleeves, leaning against the bar window-frame; his wife, looking over the little half-door; and I, in some confusion, looking up at them from outside the partition.

He saw the scene while he was an actor in it. Already the *Sketches by Boz* showed the exuberance of this power, and in his last years more than one paper in the delightful *Uncommercial Traveller* series proved it to be as inexhaustible as ever, while the art with which it was exercised had become more refined. Who has better described (for who was more sensitive to it?) the mysterious influence of crowds, and who the pitiful pathos of solitude? Who has ever surpassed Dickens in his representations, varied a thousandfold, but still appealing to the same emotions, common to us all, of the crises or turning-points of human life? Who has dwelt with a more potent effect on that catastrophe which the drama of every human life must reach; whose scenes of death in its pathetic, pitiful, reverend, terrible, ghastly forms speak more to the imagination and more to the heart? There is,

however, one species of scenes in which the genius of
Dickens seems to me to exercise a still stronger spell—
those which *precede* a catastrophe, which are charged like
thunderclouds with the coming storm.   And here the constructive art is at work; for it is the arrangement of the
incidents, past and to come, combined by anticipation in
the mind of the reader, which gives their extraordinary
force to such scenes as the nocturnal watching of Nancy
by Noah, or Carker's early walk to the railway station,
where he is to meet his doom.   Extremely powerful,
too, in a rather different way, is the scene in *Little Dorrit*,
described in a word or two, of the parting of Bar and
Physician at dawn, after they have "found out Mr.
Merdle's complaint : "

> Before parting, at Physician's door, they both looked up at
> the sunny morning sky, into which the smoke of a few early fires,
> and the breath and voices of a few early stirrers, were peacefully
> rising, and then looked round upon the immense city, and said :
> "If all those hundreds and thousands of beggared people who
> were yet asleep could only know, as they two spoke, the ruin
> that impended over them, what a fearful cry against one
> miserable soul would go up to Heaven!"

Nor is it awe only, but pity also, which he is able thus
to move beforehand, as in *Dombey and Son*, in the incomparable scenes leading up to little Paul's death.

More diverse opinions have been expressed as to
Dickens' mastery of that highest part of the novelist's
art, which we call characterisation.   Undoubtedly, the
characters which he draws are included in a limited range.
Yet I question whether their range can be justly termed
narrow as compared with that commanded by any other
great English novelist except Scott, or with those of
many novelists of other literatures except Balzac.   But

within his own range Dickens is unapproached. His novels do not altogether avoid the common danger of uninteresting heroes and insipid heroines ; but only a very few of his heroes are conventionally declamatory like Nicholas Nickleby, and few of his heroines simper sentimentally like Rose Maylie. Nor can I for a moment assent to the condemnation which has been pronounced upon all the female characters in Dickens' books, as more or less feeble or artificial. At the same time it is true that from women of a mightier mould Dickens' imagination turns aside; he could not have drawn a Dorothea Casaubon any more than he could have drawn Romola herself. Similarly, heroes of the chivalrous or magnanimous type, representatives of generous effort in a great cause, will not easily be met with in his writings : he never even essayed the picture of an artist devoted to art for her own sake.

It suited the genius, and in later years perhaps the temper, of Dickens as an author, to leave out of sight those " public virtues " to which no man was in truth less blind than himself, and to remain content with the illustration of types of the private or domestic kind. We may cheerfully take to us the censure that our great humorist was in nothing more English than in this—that his sympathy with the affections of the hearth and the home knew almost no bounds. A symbolisation of this may be found in the honour which, from the *Sketches* and *Pickwick* onwards through a long series of Christmas books and Christmas Numbers, Dickens, doubtless very consciously, paid to the one great festival of English family life. Yet so far am I from agreeing with those critics who think that he is hereby lowered to the level of the poets of the teapot and the plum-pudding, that I am at a loss how to express my admiration for this side of his genius—tender with the tenderness of Cowper, playful with the playfulness of Goldsmith, natural with the naturalness of the author of *Amelia.* Who was ever more at home with children than he, and, for that matter, with babies to begin with? Mr. Horne relates how he once heard a lady exclaim : "Oh, do read to us about the baby ; Dickens is capital at a baby!" Even when most playful, most farcical concerning children, his fun is rarely without something of true tenderness, for he knew the meaning of that dreariest solitude which he has so often pictured, but nowhere, of course, with a truthfulness going so straight to the heart as in *David Copperfield*—the solitude of a child left to itself. Another wonderfully true child-character is that of Pip in *Great Expectations,* who is also, as his years progress, an admirable study of boy-nature. For Dickens thoroughly understood what that mysterious variety of humankind really is, and was always, if one may so say, on the look-out for him. He knew him in the brightness and freshness which makes true *ingénus* of such delightful characters (rare enough in fiction) as Walter Gay and Mrs. Lirriper's grandson. He knew him in his festive mood—witness the amusing letter in which he describes a water-expedition at Eton with his son and two of his irrepressible schoolfellows. He knew him in his precocity—the boy of about three feet high at the George and Vulture, "in a hairy cap and fustian overalls, whose garb bespoke a laudable ambition to attain in time the elevation of an hostler ; " and the thing on the roof of the Harrisburg coach, which, when the rain was over, slowly upreared itself, and patronisingly piped out the inquiry : "Well now, stranger, I guess you find this a'most like an English arternoon, hey ?" He knew the Gavroche who danced attendance on Mr. Quilp at his wharf, and those strangest, but by no means least true, types of all, the pupil-teachers in Mr. Fagin's academy.

But these, with the exception of the last-named, which show much shrewd and kindly insight into the paradoxes of human nature, are of course the mere *croquis* of the great humorist's pencil. His men and women, and the passions, the desires, the loves, and hatreds that agitate them, he has usually chosen to depict on that background of domestic life which is in a greater or less degree common to us all. And it is thus also that he has secured to him-self the vast public which vibrates very differently from a mere class or section of society to the touch of a popular speaker or writer. "The more," he writes, "we see of life and its brevity, and the world and its varieties, the more we know that no exercise of our abilities in any art, but the addressing of it to the great ocean of humanity in which we are drops, and not to bye-ponds (very stagnant) here and there, ever can or ever will lay the foundations of an endurable retrospect." The types of character which in his fictions he chiefly delights in reproducing are accord-ingly those which most of us have opportunities enough of comparing with the realities around us; and this test, a sound one within reasonable limits, was the test he de-manded. To no other author were his own characters ever more real; and Forster observes, that "what he had most to notice in Dickens at the very outset of his career, was his indifference to any praise of his performances on the merely literary side, compared with the higher recognition of them as bits of actual life, with the meaning and purpose, on their part, and the responsibility on his, of realities, rather than creations of fancy." It is, then, the favourite growths of our own age and country for which we shall most readily

story is disagreeable, and not merely the fictitious form."
His economy is less strict with characters of the opposite
class, true copies of Nature's own handiwork—the Tom
Pinches and Trotty Vecks and Clara Peggottys, who
reconcile us with our kind, and Mr. Pickwick himself,
"a human being replete with benevolence," to borrow a
phrase from a noble passage in Dickens' most congenial
predecessor. These characters in Dickens have a warmth
which only the creations of Fielding and Smollett had
possessed before, and which, like these old masters, he
occasionally carries to excess. At the other extreme stand
those characters in which the art of Dickens, always in
union with the promptings of his moral nature, illustrates
the mitigating or redeeming qualities observable even in
the outcasts of our civilisation. To me his figures of this
kind, when they are not too intensely elaborated, are not
the least touching; and there is something as pathetic
in the uncouth convict Magwitch as in the consumptive
crossing-sweeper Jo.

As a matter of course, it is possible to take exceptions
of one kind or another to some of the characters created
by Dickens in so extraordinary a profusion. I hardly
know of any other novelist less obnoxious to the charge
of repeating himself; though, of course, many characters
in his earlier or shorter works contained in themselves
the germs of later and fuller developments. But Bob
Sawyer and Dick Swiveller, Noah Claypole and Uriah
Heep are at least sufficiently independent variations on
the same themes. On the other hand, Filer and Cute,
in *The Chimes*, were the first sketches of Gradgrind and
Bounderby, in *Hard Times*, and Clemency in *The Battle
of Life*, prefigures Peggotty in *David Copperfield*. No one
could seriously quarrel with such repetitions as these, and

there are remarkably few of them; for the fertile genius
of Dickens took delight in the variety of its creativeness,
and, as if to exemplify this, there was no relation upon
the contrasted humours of which he better loved to dwell
than that of partnership. It has been seen how rarely
his inventive power condescended to supplement itself
by what in the novel corresponds to the mimicry of the
stage, and what in truth is as degrading to the one as it
is to the other—the reproduction of originals *from real
life*. On the other hand, he carries his habit too far of
making a particular phrase do duty as an index of a
character. This trick also is a trick of the stage, where
it often enough makes the judicious grieve. Many may
be inclined to censure it in Dickens as one of several
forms of the exaggeration which is so frequently
condemned in him. There was no charge to which
he was more sensitive; and in the preface to *Martin
Chuzzlewit* he accordingly (not for the first time)
turned round upon the objectors, declaring roundly
that "what is exaggeration to one class of minds
and perceptions is plain truth to another;" and
hinting a doubt "whether it is *always* the writer who
colours highly, or whether it is now and then the reader
whose eye for colour is a little dull." I certainly do not
think that the term "exaggerated" is correctly applied to
such conventional characters of sensational romance
as Rosa Dartle, who has, as it were, lost her way into
David Copperfield, while Hortense and Madame Defarge
seem to be in their proper places in *Bleak House*, and *A
Tale of Two Cities*. In his earlier writings, and in the
fresher and less overcharged serious parts of his later
books, he rarely if ever paints black in black; even the
Jew Fagin has a moment of relenting against the sleeping

Oliver; he is not that unreal thing, a "demon," whereas
Sikes is that real thing, a brute.   On the other hand,
certainly he at times makes his characters more laughable
than nature; few great humorists have so persistently
sought to efface the line which separates the barely possible
from the morally probable.   This was, no doubt, largely
due to his inclination towards the grotesque, which a
severer literary training might have taught him to restrain;
thus he liked to introduce insane or imbecile personages
into fiction, where, as in real life, they are often dangerous
to handle.   It is to his sense of the grotesque, rather than
to any deep-seated satirical intention, and certainly not to
any want of reverence or piety in his very simple and very
earnest nature, that I would likewise ascribe the exaggera
tion and unfairness of which he is guilty against Little
Bethel and all its works.   But in this, as in other instances, no form of humour requires more delicate
handling than the grotesque, and none is more liable
to cause fatigue.   Latterly, Dickens was always adding
to his gallery of eccentric portraits, and, if inner currents
may be traced by outward signs, it may be worth while
to apply the test of his *names*, which become more and
more odd as their owners deviate more and more from the
path of nature.   Who more simply and yet more happily
named than the leading members of the Pickwick Club—
from the poet, Mr. Snodgrass, to the sportsman, Mr.
Winkle—Nathaniel, not Daniel; but with Veneering and
Lammle, and Boffin and Venus, and Crisparkle and
Grewgious—be they actual names or not—we feel instinctively that we are in the region of the transnormal.

Lastly, in their descriptive power and the faithfulness
with which they portray the life and ways of particular
periods or countries, of special classes, professions, or other

divisions of mankind, the books of Dickens are, again of
course within their range, unequalled. He sought his
materials chiefly at home, though his letters from Italy
and Switzerland and America, and his French pictures in
sketch and story, show how much wider a field his
descriptive powers might have covered. The *Sketches by
Boz* and the *Pickwick Papers* showed a mastery, unsurpassed before or since, in the description of the life of
English society in its middle and lower classes, and in
Oliver Twist he lifted the curtain from some of the
rotten parts of our civilisation. This history of a workhouse child also sounded the note of that sympathy with
the poor which gave to Dickens' descriptions of their
sufferings and their struggles a veracity beyond mere
accuracy of detail. He was still happier in describing
their household virtues, their helpfulness to one another,
their compassion for those who are the poorest of all—the
friendless and the outcast—as he did in his *Old Curiosity
Shop*, and in most of his Christmas books. His pictures
of middle-class life abounded in kindly humour; but the
humour and pathos of poverty—more especially the
poverty which has not yet lost its self-respect—commended
themselves most of all to his descriptive power. Where,
as in *Nicholas Nickleby* and later works, he essayed to
describe the manners of the higher classes, he was, as a
rule, far less successful : partly because there was in his
nature a vein of rebellion against the existing system of
society, so that except in his latest books, he usually
approached a description of members of its dominant orders
with a satirical intention, or at least an undertone of bitterness. At the same time, I demur to the common assertion
that Dickens could not draw a real gentleman. All that
can be said is that it very rarely suited his purpose to do so,
supposing the term to include manners as well as feelings

and actions ; though Mr. Twemlow, in *Our Mutual Friend*, might be instanced as a (perhaps rather conscious) exception of one kind, and Sir Leicester Dedlock, in the latter part of *Bleak House*, as another. Moreover, a closer examination of Lord Frederick Verisopht and Cousin Feenix will show that, gull as the one, and ninny as the other is, neither has anything that can be called ungentlemanly about him ; on the contrary, the characters, on the whole, rather plead in favour of the advantage than of the valuelessness of blue blood. As for Dickens' other noblemen, whom I find enumerated in an American dictionary of his characters, they are nearly all mere passing embodiments of satirical fancies, which pretend to be nothing more.

Another ingenious enthusiast has catalogued the numerous callings, professions, and trades of the person·ages appearing in Dickens' works I cannot agree with the criticism that in his personages the man is apt to become forgotten in the externals of his calling—the barrister's wig and gown, as it were, standing for the barrister, and the beadle's cocked hat and staff for the beadle. But he must have possessed in its perfection the curious detective faculty of deducing a man's occupation from his manners. To him nothing wore a neutral tint, and no man or woman was featureless. He was, it should be remembered, always observing ; half his life he was afoot. When he undertook to describe any novel or unfamiliar kind of manners, he spared no time or trouble in making a special study of his subject. He was not content to know the haunts of the London thieves by hearsay, or to read the history of opium-smoking and its effects in Blue-books. From the office of his journal in London, we find him starting on these self-imposed commissions, and from his hotel in New York. The whole art of descriptive reporting, which has no doubt produced a

large quantity of trashy writing, but has also been of real
service in arousing a public interest in neglected corners
of our social life, was, if not actually set on foot, at any
rate reinvigorated and vitalised by him. No one was so
delighted to notice the oddities which habit and tradition
stereotype in particular classes of men; a complete natural
history of the country actor, the London landlady, and the
British waiter might be compiled from his pages. This
power of observation and description extended from human
life to that of animals. His habits of life could not but
make him the friend of dogs, and there is some reason for
a title which was bestowed on him in a paper in a London
magazine concerning his own dogs—the Landseer of Fiction. His letters are full of delightful details concerning
these friends and companions, Turk, Linda, and the rest
of them; nor is the family of their fictitious counterparts,
culminating (intellectually) in Merrylegs, less numerous and
delightful. Cats were less congenial to Dickens, perhaps
because he had no objection to changing house; and they
appear in his works in no more attractive form than as
the attendant spirits of Mrs. Pipchin and of Mr. Krook.
But for the humours of animals in general he had a
wonderfully quick eye. Of his ravens I have already
spoken. The pony Whisker is the type of kind old
gentlemen's ponies. In one of his letters occurs an admirably droll description of the pig-market at Boulogne;
and the best unscientific description ever given of a spider
was imagined by Dickens at Broadstairs, when in his
solitude he thought

of taming spiders, as Baron Trenck did. There is one in my
cell (with a speckled body and twenty-two very decided knees)
who seems to know me.

In everything, whether animate or inanimate, he found
out at once the characteristic feature, and reproduced it in

words of faultless precision.   This is the real secret of his
descriptive power, the exercise of which it would be easy
to pursue through many other classes of subjects.   Scenery,
for its own sake, he rarely cared to describe; but no one
better understood how to reproduce the combined effect
of scenery and weather on the predisposed mind.   Thus
London and its river in especial are, as I have said,
haunted by the memory of Dickens' books.   To me it was
for years impossible to pass near London Bridge at night,
or to idle in the Temple on summer days, or to frequent
a hundred other localities on or near the Thames, without
instinctively recalling pictures scattered through the works
of Dickens—in this respect, also, a real *liber veritatis*.

Thus, and in many ways which it would be labour lost
to attempt to describe, and by many a stroke or touch of
genius which it would be idle to seek to reproduce in
paraphrase, the most observing and the most imaginative
of our English humorists revealed to us that infinite
multitude of associations which binds men together, and
makes us members one of another.   But though observation and imagination might discern and discover these
associations, sympathy—the sympathy of a generous
human heart with humanity—alone could breathe into
them the warmth of life.   Happily, to most men, there
is one place consecrated above others to the feelings of
love and goodwill; "that great altar where the worst
among us sometimes perform the worship of the heart,
and where the best have offered up such sacrifices and
done such deeds of heroism as, chronicled, would put
the proudest temples of old time, with all their vaunt-
ing annals, to the blush."   It was thus that Dickens
spoke of the sanctity of *home*; and, English in many
things, he was most English in that love of home to which
he was never weary of testifying.   But, though the " path-

way of the sublime "may have been closed to him, he knew well enough that the interests of a people and the interests of humanity are mightier than the domestic loves and cares of any man; and he conscientiously addressed himself, as to the task of his life, to the endeavour to knit humanity together. The method which he, by instinct and by choice, more especially pursued was that of seeking to show the "good in everything." This it is that made him, unreasonably sometimes, ignobly never, the champion of the poor, the helpless, the outcast. He was often tempted into a rhetoric too loud and too shrill, into a satire neither fine nor fair; for he was impatient, but not impatient of what he thought true and good. His purpose, however, was worthy of his powers; nor is there recorded among the lives of English men of letters any more single-minded in its aim, and more successful in the pursuit of it, than his. He was much criticised in his lifetime; and he will, I am well aware, be often criticised in the future by keener and more capable judges than myself. They may miss much in his writings that I find in them; but, unless they find one thing there, it were better that they never opened one of his books. He has indicated it himself when criticising a literary performance by a clever writer:

In this little MS. everything is too much patronised and condescended to, whereas the slightest touch of feeling for the rustic who is of the earth earthy, or of sisterhood with the homely servant who has made her face shine in her desire to please, would make a difference that the writer can generally imagine without trying it. You don't want any sentiment laboriously made out in such a thing. You don't want any maudlin show of it. But you do want a pervading suggestion that it is there.

The sentiment which Dickens means is the salt which will give a fresh savour of their own to his works so long as our language endures.

THE END.

INDEX

A

B

C

R. CLAY AND SONS, LTD., BREAD ST. HILL, E.C., AND BUNGAY, SUFFOLK.

English Men of Letters.

NEW SERIES.

Crown 8vo.   Gilt tops.   Flat backs.   2s. net per vol.

FORTHCOMING VOLUMES.

JAMES THOMSON. By G. C. MACAULAY.

MRS. GASKELL. By CLEMENT SHORTER.

CHARLES KINGSLEY. By G. K. CHESTERTON.

BEN JONSON. By Professor GREGORY SMITH.

WILLIAM MORRIS. By ALFRED NOYES.

VOLUMES NOW READY.

GEORGE ELIOT. By Sir LESLIE STEPHEN, K.C.B.

Mr. HERBERT PAUL in the *NINETEENTH CENTURY.*—"The first of English living critics has been fitly chosen to inaugurate the new series of Messrs. Macmillan's 'English Men of Letters.' Mr. Leslie Stephen's 'George Eliot' is a grave, sober, and measured estimate of a great Englishwoman."

Mr. W. L. COURTNEY in the *DAILY TELEGRAPH.*—"One of the most fascinating and accomplished pieces of criticism that have appeared for some time past. Mr. Stephen is a prince of contemporary critics, and any one who ventures to disagree with him incurs a very heavy responsibility."

WILLIAM HAZLITT. By AUGUSTINE BIRRELL, K.C.

ACADEMY.—"We have read this book through in a single sitting, delighted by its easy yet careful narrative, its sane and kindly comment, and last, not least, by its wealth of quotation."

DAILY NEWS.—"Mr. Birrell has made judicious use of the mass of materials at his disposal, and with the aid of his acute and thoughtful running commentary, has enabled his readers to form a tolerably accurate and complete conception of the brilliant essayist and critic with no greater expenditure of time and pains than is needed for the perusal of this slender volume."

MATTHEW ARNOLD. By HERBERT PAUL.

Canon AINGER in the *PILOT.*—"A most interesting and admirably written estimate of Matthew Arnold. This estimate, so far as regards Mr. Arnold's poetry and his prose critical essays, seems to me so nearly faultless as hardly to justify any counter criticism."

WESTMINSTER GAZETTE.—"An exceedingly effective essay in criticism."

SPECTATOR.—"This monograph is valuable as a succinct statement, set out in an appreciative, interesting, skilful, and sometimes sparkling fashion, of the labours and pursuits that make up the tireless life of the great poet and essayist."

JOHN RUSKIN. By FREDERIC HARRISON.

TIMES.—"Mr. Harrison knew Ruskin at his best; lectured with him at the Working Men's College; visited him at Denmark Hill; and in later years often saw and corresponded with him. The result is a study of the writer marked in equal measure by discrimination and sympathy; and a picture of the man, vivid and arresting."

GLOBE.—"The best account of Ruskin and his work which has yet been given to the world. The writer is sure of his facts, and is able to illuminate them by means not only of a close personal acquaintance with his subject, but also of a wide and deep knowledge of many other men and things."

TENNYSON. By Sir ALFRED LYALL, K.C.B.

TIMES.—"The criticism is always sane, and sometimes brilliant ; it never errs on the side of exuberance ; and it is expressed in excellent English, moulded into dignified paragraphs."

DAILY TELEGRAPH.—"The memoir is admirably carried out, telling the reader precisely what he wants to know, giving an account of what the poems contain, as well as a running commentary upon their character and value, being written, in short, not for the superior person, but for the average man of the world with literary tastes."

SAMUEL RICHARDSON. By AUSTIN DOBSON.

TIMES.—"Mr. Austin Dobson has written what is very nearly a perfect little book of its kind."

Mr. W. L. COURTNEY in the *DAILY TELEGRAPH.*—"Mr. Dobson's study is absolutely in the first rank, worthy to be put by the side of Sir Leslie Stephen's criticism of George Eliot."

BROWNING. By G. K. CHESTERTON.

TIMES.—"The originality and suggestiveness of Mr. Chesterton's work . . . his sanity and virility of temper are evident and refreshing."

Mr. W. L. COURTNEY in the *DAILY TELEGRAPH.*—"One of the most illuminating and stimulating pieces of work which have been produced in our not wholly critical age."

CRABBE. By ALFRED AINGER.

TIMES.—"Canon Ainger has given us the book we should expect from him, one full of sincerity, good taste, and good sense. The story of the poet's uneventful life is admirably retold, with the quiet distinction of a style which is intent on its own business, and too sure of producing its effect to care about forcing attention by rhetorical or epigrammatic fireworks. And Canon Ainger has been fortunate enough to be able to add a few new facts, and throw a little new light on the poet's life."

FANNY BURNEY. By AUSTIN DOBSON.

TIMES.—"A book of unfailing charm—perhaps the most charming of this admirable series."

GLOBE.—"Eloquent and sparkling."

JEREMY TAYLOR. By EDMUND GOSSE.

ACADEMY.—"A worthy monument to one of the greatest of Anglican divines."

MORNING POST.—"His profound and brilliant study of Jeremy Taylor's life and writings."

ROSSETTI. By ARTHUR C. BENSON.

TIMES.—"A very good book, full of well-chosen facts and of discreet sympathy with a character that needs a good deal of understanding."

PILOT.—"Mr. Benson displays not only a delicate sympathy, but a penetration and a sanity of judgment that enable him to put before us not merely a plausible, but a convincing portrait of a man who twenty years after his death, in spite of changing fashions, exercises, as in his own day, a strange and potent spell over the imagination."

MARIA EDGEWORTH. By the Hon. EMILY LAWLESS.

GUARDIAN.—"Miss Lawless is to be congratulated upon having produced what is very nearly the ideal life of Maria Edgeworth."

GLOBE.—"A memoir of great interest."

HOBBES. By Sir LESLIE STEPHEN, K.C.B.

TIMES.—"One of the most remarkable additions to the 'Men of Letters.'"

PALL MALL GAZETTE.—"One of the happiest examples of Sir Leslie's marvellous success in making biography unfailing in its interest."

ADAM SMITH. By Francis W. Hirst.

THE WORLD.—"A careful and sympathetic survey of the life, work, and teaching of the famous political economist."

TIMES.—"Mr. Hirst's interesting sketch leaves the impression of a life singularly full, rich, and successful, lightened and warmed even towards the close by the sunshine of friendship and affection."

THOMAS MOORE. By Stephen Gwynn.

TIMES.—"An admirable book. . . . Mr. Gwynn has surely said the last word about this warm-hearted, volatile personage, whose tact and taste in writing verse were for so long mistaken for passion."

MORNING POST.—"In every way worthy of the series to which it belongs."

SYDNEY SMITH. By George W. E. Russell.

TIMES.—"Brilliant biographical study. . . . The part of the book which is Mr. Russell's own could hardly be improved for vigour, terseness, and point."

ATHENÆUM.—"Those responsible for the additional volumes in the 'English Men of Letters' Series made no mistake when they invited Mr. George Russell to undertake a study of Sydney Smith."

EDWARD FITZGERALD. By Arthur C. Benson.

DAILY TELEGRAPH.—"It is not too much to say that this volume will rank as one of the very best of the remarkable series to which it belongs."

STANDARD.—"His sketch is the most satisfactory picture of Fitzgerald that we possess. It is informed by a fine critical judgment, and by the tolerant sympathy which is above all things necessary in dealing with this shy, eccentric personality."

ANDREW MARVELL. By Augustine Birrell, K.C.

DAILY GRAPHIC.—"Himself a satirist and a member of Parliament, no one is better able to form an accurate judgment of Marvell than his latest and, we think, best biographer."

DAILY NEWS.—"A delightful piece of work."

SIR THOMAS BROWNE. By Edmund Gosse.

TIMES.—"This is very skilful biography; very intelligent criticism."

WORLD.—"This book is one of the best of the series."

WALTER PATER. By Arthur C. Benson.

ATHENÆUM.—"The life of Pater could not have fallen into safer, kindlier, or more sympathetic keeping than that of Mr. Arthur Benson; and a series of biographies which maintains a high level is to be congratulated on a volume really excellent of its kind."

GUARDIAN.—"The book is one which no student of modern literature should fail to read."

SHAKESPEARE. By Walter Raleigh.

TIMES.—"Professor Raleigh has given us an essay overflowing with life, crammed with suggestion, full of stimulating ideas and happy turns of phrase, and with no dull page from beginning to end."

Professor Dowden in *THE NATION.*—"Professor Raleigh has felt over again, with penetrative imagination and fine intelligence, the beauty and the greatness of Shakespeare's poetry; he has placed these in their proper environment, and, by virtue of a rare charm of style, enabled us to see with his eyes a most harmonious vision. . . . A wise and beautiful book."

English Men of Letters.

EDITED BY JOHN MORLEY.

RE-ISSUE OF THE ORIGINAL SERIES.

LIBRARY EDITION. UNIFORM WITH THE NEW SERIES.

Crown 8vo. Gilt tops. Flat backs. 2s. net per vol

ADDISON.
By W. J. COURTHOPE.
BACON.
By Dean CHURCH.
BENTLEY.
By Sir RICHARD JEBB.
BUNYAN.
By J. A. FROUDE.
BURKE.
By JOHN MORLEY.
BURNS.
By Principal SHAIRP.
BYRON.
By Professor NICHOL.
CARLYLE.
By Professor NICHOL.
CHAUCER.
By Dr. A. W. WARD.
COLERIDGE.
By H. D. TRAILL.
COWPER.
By GOLDWIN SMITH.
DEFOE.
By W. MINTO.
DE QUINCEY.
By Professor MASSON.
DICKENS.
By Dr. A. W. WARD.
DRYDEN.
By Professor SAINTSBURY.
FIELDING.
By AUSTIN DOBSON.
GIBBON.
By J. C. MORISON.
GOLDSMITH.
By W. BLACK.
GRAY.
By EDMUND GOSSE.
HAWTHORNE.
By HENRY JAMES.

HUME.
By Professor HUXLEY, F.R.S.
JOHNSON.
By Sir LESLIE STEPHEN, K.C.B.
KEATS.
By SIDNEY COLVIN.
LAMB, CHARLES.
By Canon AINGER.
LANDOR.
By SIDNEY COLVIN.
LOCKE.
By THOMAS FOWLER.
MACAULAY.
By J. C. MORISON.
MILTON.
By MARK PATTISON.
POPE.
By Sir LESLIE STEPHEN, K.C.B.
SCOTT.
By R. H. HUTTON.
SHELLEY.
By J. A. SYMONDS.
SHERIDAN.
By Mrs. OLIPHANT.
SIDNEY.
By J. A. SYMONDS.
SOUTHEY.
By Professor DOWDEN.
SPENSER.
By Dean CHURCH.
STERNE.
By H. D. TRAILL.
SWIFT.
By Sir LESLIE STEPHEN, K.C.B.
THACKERAY.
By ANTHONY TROLLOPE.
WORDSWORTH.
By F. W. H. MYERS.

MACMILLAN AND CO., LTD., LONDON

CL. 5.12.07.